CHILD PROTECTION

KIM HOLT

D0928878

palgrave
macmillan

First published 2014 by
PALGRAVE MACMILLAN

Palgrave Macmillan in the UK is an imprint of Macmillan Publishers Limited, registered in England, company number 785998, of Houndmills, Basingstoke, Hampshire RG21 6XS.

Palgrave Macmillan in the US is a division of St Martin's Press LLC, 175 Fifth Avenue, New York, NY 10010.

Palgrave Macmillan is the global academic imprint of the above companies and has companies and representatives throughout the world.

Palgrave® and Macmillan® are registered trademarks in the United States, the United Kingdom, Europe and other countries

ISBN: 978–1–137–28667–3

This book is printed on paper suitable for recycling and made from fully managed and sustained forest sources. Logging, pulping and manufacturing processes are expected to conform to the environmental regulations of the country of origin.

A catalogue record for this book is available from the British Library.

A catalog record for this book is available from the Library of Congress.

Typeset by Cambrian Typesetters, Camberley, Surrey

Printed and bound in the UK by The Lavenham Press Ltd, Suffolk

CHILD PROTECTION

WITHDRAWN

1 MAR 2024

FOCUS ON SOCIAL WORK LAW
Series Editor: Alison Brammer

Palgrave Macmillan's Focus on Social Work Law series
accessible guides to the principles, structures and proces
of the law as they apply to social work practice. Designed consists of compact,
understanding as well as refresh practitioners' knowledgees of particular areas
focused, digestible and navigable content in an easily po to develop students'
, each book provides
Available now
table form.

Looked After Children, Caroline Ball
Child Protection, Kim Holt
Capacity and Autonomy, Robert Johns
Making Good Decisions, Michael Preston-Shoot

Forthcoming titles

Court and Legal Skills, Penny Cooper
Adoption and Permanency, Philip Musson
Youth Justice, Jo Staines
Children in Need of Support, Joanne Westwood
Safeguarding Adults, Alison Brammer

Author of the bestselling textbook *Social Work Law*, Alison Bramn.
solicitor with specialist experience working in Social Services, in
protection, adoption, mental health and community care. Alison is a qualifie
the MA in Child Care Law and Practice and the MA in Adult Safe uding chil
Keele University. oordinat
uarding a

Series Standing Order

ISBN 9781137017833 paperback
(*outside North America only*)
You can receive future titles in this series as they are published by placing
standing order. Please contact your bookseller or, in the case of difficulty, write
to us at the address below with your name and address, the title of the series
and the ISBN quoted above.
Customer Services Department, Macmillan Distribution Ltd
Houndmills, Basingstoke, Hampshire RG21 6XS, England

To my father Clifford (1932–1994) and my
mother Doreen (1934–2005) who gave so much,
and who would have been very proud.

Thank you.

CONTENTS

TABLE OF CASES

TABLE OF LEGISLATION

ACKNOWLEDGMENTS

I am particularly indebted for the advice, support and patience from my family, friends and colleagues.

ABBREVIATIONS

CA04	Children Act 2004
CA89	Children Act 1989
Cafcass	Children and Family Court Advisory and Support Service
DCA	Department for Constitutional Affairs
DCSF	Department for Children, Schools and Families
DfE	Department for Education
DfES	Department for Education and Skills
DoH	Department of Health
DHSS	Department of Health and Social Security
ECHR	European Convention on Human Rights
ECtHR	European Court of Human Rights
EPO	emergency protection order
FCA	family court advisor
FGCs	family group conferences
FPR	Family Procedure Rules
FRG	Family Rights Group
GAL	guardian ad litem
IRO	independent reviewing officer
JRT	Judicial Review Team
LSCB	Local Safeguarding Children Board
MoJ	Ministry of Justice
NSPCC	National Society for the Prevention of Cruelty to Children
PLO	*Public Law Outline*
SCR	serious case review
UNCRC	United Nations Convention on the Rights of the Child

USING THIS BOOK

Aim of the series

Welcome to the Focus on Social Work Law Series.

This introductory section aims to elucidate the aims and philosophy of the series; introduce some key themes that run through the series; outline the key features within each volume; and offer a brief legal skills guide to complement use of the series.

The Social Work Law Focus Series provides a distinct range of specialist resources for students and practitioners. Each volume provides an accessible and practical discussion of the law applicable to a particular area of practice. The length of each volume ensures that whilst portable and focused there is nevertheless a depth of coverage of each topic beyond that typically contained in comprehensive textbooks addressing all aspects of social work law and practice.

Each volume includes the relevant principles, structures and processes of the law (with case law integrated into the text) and highlights clearly the application of the law to practice. A key objective for each text is to identify the policy context of each area of practice and the factors that have shaped the law into its current presentation. As law is constantly developing and evolving, where known, likely future reform of the law is identified. Each book takes a critical approach, noting inconsistencies, omissions and other challenges faced by those charged with its implementation.

The significance of the Human Rights Act 1998 to social work practice is a common theme in each text and implications of the Act for practice in the particular area are identified with inclusion of relevant case law.

The series focuses on the law in England and Wales. Some references may be made to comparable aspects of law in Scotland and Northern Ireland, particularly to highlight differences in approach. With devolution in Scotland and the expanding role of the Welsh Assembly Government it will be important for practitioners in those areas and working at the borders to be familiar with any such differences.

Features

At a glance content lists

Each chapter begins with a bullet point list summarizing the key points within the topic included in that chapter. From this list the reader can see 'at a glance' how the materials are organized and what to expect in that section. The introductory chapter provides an overview of the book, outlining coverage in each chapter that enables the reader to see how the topic develops throughout the text. The boundaries of the discussion are set including, where relevant, explicit recognition of areas that are excluded from the text.

Key case analysis

One of the key aims of the series is to emphasize an integrated under-standing of law, comprising legislation and case law and practice. For this reason each chapter includes at least one key case analysis feature focusing on a particularly significant case. The facts of the case are outlined in brief followed by analysis of the implications of the decision for social work practice in a short commentary. Given the significance of the selected cases, readers are encouraged to follow up references and read the case in full together with any published commentaries.

On-the-spot questions

These questions are designed to consolidate learning and prompt reflection on the material considered. These questions may be used as a basis for discussion with colleagues or fellow students and may also prompt consideration or further investigation of how the law is applied within a particular setting or authority, for example, looking at information provided to service users on a council website. Questions may also follow key cases, discussion of research findings or practice scenarios, focusing on the issues raised and application of the relevant law to practice.

Practice focus

Each volume incorporates practice-focused case scenarios to demon-strate how the law is applied to social work practice. The scenarios may be fictional or based on an actual decision.

Further reading

Each chapter closes with suggestions for further reading to develop knowledge and critical understanding. Annotated to explain the reasons for inclusion, the reader may be directed to classic influential pieces, such as enquiry reports, up-to-date research and analysis of issues discussed in the chapter, and relevant policy documents. In addition students may wish to read in full the case law included throughout the text and to follow up references integrated into discussion of each topic.

Websites

As further important sources of information, websites are also included in the text with links from the companion website. Some may be a gateway to access significant documents including government publications, others may provide accessible information for service users or present a particular perspective on an area, such as the voices of experts by experience. Given the rapid development of law and practice across the range of topics covered in the series, reference to relevant websites can be a useful way to keep pace with actual and anticipated changes.

Glossary

Each text includes a subject-specific glossary of key terms for quick reference and clarification. A flashcard version of the glossary is available on the companion website.

Visual aids

As appropriate, visual aids are included where information may be presented accessibly as a table, graph or flow chart. This approach is particularly helpful for the presentation of some complex areas of law and to demonstrate structured decision-making or options available.

Companion site

The series-wide companion site www.palgrave.com/socialworklaw provides additional learning resources, including flashcard glossaries, web links, a legal skills guide, and a blog to communicate important developments and updates. The site will also host a student feedback zone.

Key sources of law

In this section an outline of the key sources of law considered through-out the series is provided. The following 'Legal skills' section includes some guidance on the easiest ways to access and understand these sources.

Legislation

The term legislation is used interchangeably with Acts of Parliament and statutes to refer to primary sources of law.

All primary legislation is produced through the parliamentary process, beginning its passage as a Bill. Bills may have their origins as an expressed policy in a government manifesto, in the work of the Law Commission, or following and responding to a significant event such as a child death or the work of a government department such as the Home Office.

Each Bill is considered by both the House of Lords and House of Commons, debated and scrutinized through various committee stages before becoming an Act on receipt of royal assent.

Legislation has a title and year, for example, the Equality Act 2010. Legislation can vary in length from an Act with just one section to others with over a hundred. Lengthy Acts are usually divided into headed 'Parts' (like chapters) containing sections, subsections and paragraphs. For example, s. 31 of the Children Act 1989 is in Part IV entitled 'Care and Supervision' and outlines the criteria for care order applications. Beyond the main body of the Act the legislation may also include 'Schedules' following the main provisions. Schedules have the same force of law as the rest of the Act but are typically used to cover detail such as a list of legislation which has been amended or revoked by the current Act or detailed matters linked to a specific provision, for instance, Schedule 2 of the Children Act 1989 details specific services (e.g. day centres) which may be provided under the duty to safeguard and promote the welfare of children in need, contained in s. 17.

Remember also that statutes often contain sections dealing with inter-pretation or definitions and, although often situated towards the end of the Act, these can be a useful starting point.

Legislation also includes Statutory Instruments which may be in the form of rules, regulations and orders. The term delegated legislation collectively describes this body of law as it is made under delegated authority of Parliament, usually by a minister or government department. Statutory Instruments tend to provide additional detail to the outline scheme provided by the primary legislation, the Act of Parliament. Statutory Instruments are usually cited by year and a number, for example, Local Authority Social Services (Complaints Procedure) Order SI 2006/1681.

Various documents may be issued to further assist with the implementation of legislation including guidance and codes of practice.

Guidance

Guidance documents may be described as formal or practice guidance. Formal guidance may be identified as such where it is stated to have been issued under s. 7(1) of the Local Authority Social Services Act 1970, which provides that 'local authorities shall act under the general guidance of the Secretary of State'. An example of s. 7 guidance is *Working Together to Safeguard Children* (2013, London: Department of Health). The significance of s. 7 guidance was explained by Sedley J in *R v London Borough of Islington, ex parte Rixon* [1997] ELR 66: 'Parliament in enacting s. 7(1) did not intend local authorities to whom ministerial guidance was given to be free, having considered it, to take it or leave it ... in my view parliament by s. 7(1) has required local authorities to follow the path charted by the Secretary of State's guidance, with liberty to deviate from it where the local authority judges on admissible grounds that there is good reason to do so, but without freedom to take a substantially different course.' (71)

Practice guidance does not carry s. 7 status but should nevertheless normally be followed as setting examples of what good practice might look like.

Codes of practice

Codes of practice have been issued to support the Mental Health Act 1983 and the Mental Capacity Act 2005. Again, it is a matter of good practice to follow the recommendations of the codes and these lengthy documents include detailed and illustrative scenarios to assist with interpretation and application of the legislation. There may also be a duty on specific people charged with responsibilities under the primary legislation to have regard to the code.

Guidance and codes of practice are available on relevant websites, for example, the Department of Health, as referenced in individual volumes.

Case law

Case law provides a further major source of law. In determining disputes in court the judiciary applies legislation. Where provisions within legislation are unclear or ambiguous the judiciary follows principles of statutory interpretation but at times judges are quite creative.

Some areas of law are exclusively contained in case law and described as common law. Most law of relevance to social work practice is of relatively recent origin and has its primary basis in legislation. Case law remains relevant as it links directly to such legislation and may clarify and explain provisions and terminology within the legislation. The significance of a particular decision will depend on the position of the court in a hierarchy whereby the Supreme Court is most senior and the magistrates' court is junior. Decisions of the higher courts bind the lower courts – they must be followed. This principle is known as the doctrine of precedent. Much legal debate takes place as to the precise element of a ruling which subsequently binds other decisions. This is especially the case where in the Court of Appeal or Supreme Court there are between three and five judges hearing a case, majority judgments are allowed and different judges may arrive at the same conclusion but for different reasons. Where a judge does not agree with the majority, the term dissenting judgment is applied.

It is important to understand how cases reach court. Many cases in social work law are based on challenges to the way a local authority has exercised its powers. This is an aspect of administrative law known as judicial review where the central issue for the court is not the substance of the decision taken by the authority but the way it was taken. Important considerations will be whether the authority has exceeded its powers, failed to follow established procedures or acted irrationally.

Before an individual can challenge an authority in judicial review it will usually be necessary to exhaust other remedies first, including local authority complaints procedures. If unsatisfied with the outcome of a complaint an individual has a further option which is to complain to the local government ombudsman (LGO). The LGO investigates alleged cases of maladministration and may make recommendations to local authorities including the payment of financial compensation. Ombudsman decisions may be accessed on the LGO website and make interesting reading. In cases involving social services, a common concern across children's and adults' services is unreasonable delay in carrying out assessments and providing services. See www.lgo.org.uk.

Classification of law

The above discussion related to the sources and status of laws. It is also important to note that law can serve a variety of functions and may be grouped into recognized classifications. For law relating to social work practice key classifications distinguish between law which is criminal or civil and law which is public or private.

Whilst acknowledging the importance of these classifications, it must also be appreciated that individual concerns and circumstances may not always fall so neatly into the same categories, a given scenario may engage with criminal, civil, public and private law.

- Criminal law relates to alleged behaviour which is defined by statute or common law as an offence prosecuted by the state, carrying a penalty which may include imprisonment. The offence must be proved 'beyond reasonable doubt'.
- Civil law is the term applied to all other areas of law and often focuses on disputes between individuals. A lower standard of proof, 'balance of probabilities', applies in civil cases.
- Public law is that in which society has some interest and involves a public authority, such as care proceedings.
- Private law operates between individuals, such as marriage or contract.

Legal skills guide: accessing and understanding the law

Legislation

Legislation may be accessed as printed copies published by The Stationery Office and is also available online. Some books on a particular area of law will include a copy of the Act (sometimes annotated) and this is a useful way of learning about new laws. As time goes by, however, and amendments are made to legislation it can become increasingly difficult to keep track of the up-to-date version of an Act. Revised and up-to-date versions of legislation (as well as the version originally enacted) are available on the website www.legislation.gov.uk.

Legislation may also be accessed on the Parliament website. Here, it is possible to trace the progress of current and draft Bills and a link to Hansard provides transcripts of debates on Bills as they pass through both Houses of Parliament, www.parliament.uk.

Bills and new legislation are often accompanied by 'Explanatory notes' which can give some background to the development of the new law and offer useful explanations of each provision.

Case law

Important cases are reported in law reports available in traditional bound volumes (according to court, specialist area or general weekly reports) or online. Case referencing is known as citation and follows particular conventions according to whether a hard copy law report or online version is sought.

Citation of cases in law reports begins with the names of the parties, followed by the year and volume number of the law report, followed by an abbreviation of the law report title, then the page number. For example: *Lawrence v Pembrokeshire CC* [2007] 2 FLR 705. The case is reported in volume 2 of the 2007 Family Law Report at page 705.

Online citation, sometimes referred to as neutral citation because it is not linked to a particular law report, also starts with the names of the parties, followed by the year in which the case was decided, followed by an abbreviation of the court in which the case was heard, followed by a number representing the place in the order of cases decided by that court. For example: *R (Macdonald) v Royal Borough of Kensington and Chelsea* [2011] UKSC 33. Neutral citation of this case shows that it was a 2011 decision of the Supreme Court.

University libraries tend to have subscriptions to particular legal databases, such as 'Westlaw', which can be accessed by those enrolled as students, often via direct links from the university library webpage. Westlaw and LexisNexis are especially useful as sources of case law, statutes and other legal materials. Libraries usually have their own guides to these sources, again often published on their websites. For most cases there is a short summary or analysis as well as the full transcript.

As not everyone using the series will be enrolled at a university, the following website can be accessed without any subscription: BAILLI (British and Irish Legal Information Institute) www.bailii.org. This site includes judgments from the full range of UK court services including the Supreme Court, Court of Appeal and High Court but also features a wide range of tribunal decisions. Judgments for Scotland, Northern Ireland and the Republic of Ireland are also available as are judgments of the European Court of Human Rights.

Whether accessed via a law report or online, the presentation of cases follows a template. The report begins with the names of the parties, the court which heard the cases, names(s) of the judges(s) and dates of the hearing. This is followed by a summary of key legal issues involved in the case (often in italics) known as catchwords, then the headnote, which is a paragraph or so stating the key facts of the case and the nature of the claim or dispute or the criminal charge. 'HELD' indicates the ruling of the court. This is followed by a list of cases that were referred to in legal argument during the hearing, a summary of the journey of the case through appeal processes, names of the advocates and then the start of the full judgment(s) given by the judge(s). The judgment usually recounts the circumstances of the case, findings of fact and findings on the law and reasons for the decision.

If stuck on citations the Cardiff Index to Legal Abbreviations is a useful resource at www.legalabbrevs.cardiff.ac.uk.

There are numerous specific guides to legal research providing more detailed examination of legal materials but the best advice on developing legal skills is to start exploring the above and to read some case law – it's surprisingly addictive!

INTRODUCTION

AT A GLANCE THIS CHAPTER COVERS:

♦ historical overview of child care law
♦ the current child protection system
♦ reforms

Evolution of child care law

The origins of child care law date back to the late sixteenth century. The Poor Laws gave power to the boards of Poor Law guardians to provide for the destitute, including children. The Prevention of Cruelty to and Protection of Children Act 1889 was the first statute to impose criminal penalties for the mistreatment of children. Although the language used in **child protection** has evolved over the years, much of our current legislation has retained its origins from early legislation. The Children and Young Persons Act 1933 embodied many of the principles established in 1889; schedule 1 of the Act lists all the offences against children and, despite subsequent legislative reform in this area, it is still often referred to in identifying risk. The term 'boarding out' has its origins in nineteenth-century practice whereby children were 'boarded out' with other families within the community – it is only relatively recently that we have replaced the term 'boarding-out visits' with 'statutory visits', even though the duties and responsibilities of the Poor Law guardians were taken over by the local authorities in 1929.

The **welfare principle** embedded in the Children Act 1989 (CA89) was originally introduced as an overriding factor in 1886 and in 1891 courts were given the power for the first time to consult the wishes of the child. Finally, in 1925 the principle of equality of rights between mothers and fathers was enshrined in law, reflecting the prevailing ethos that the welfare of the child was the court's paramount consideration.

The Curtis Report published in 1946 was pivotal in changing the legislative landscape for child care law, which culminated in the Children Act 1948. Local authorities were subsequently tasked with providing a professional service for children. Prior to the implementation of this legislation, the majority of welfare services were provided by religious and voluntary organizations. The newly formed children's departments worked to keep children in their families, and the Children and Young Persons Act 1963 introduced the powers and duties to '*make available such advice, assistance and guidance as may promote the welfare of children by diminishing the need to receive children into or keep them in care*' (s. 1).

Furthermore, the Children and Young Persons Act 1969 introduced compulsory measures for local authorities, requiring them to intervene and assume the parental rights of a child. This legislation bolstered the concepts of 'care and control' with the result that children engaged in criminal activity could be made subject of **care orders**. In 1971, following the Seebohm Report (1969), the Local Authority Social Services Act 1970 brought together the different areas of social work practice into generic social services departments. Concern in the early 1970s about the 'drift' of planning for children in voluntary care and the need for children to be parented in permanent families stimulated the introduction of both the Children Act 1975 and the Adoption Act 1976.

The welfare principle with its origins in the late sixteenth century quite appropriately continues to feature when the court is making important decisions about the child as evident below in *Re G (A Child)* [2013].

> **KEY CASE ANALYSIS**

Re G (A Child) [2013]

The case involved a mother who had on two occasions abandoned her child. The mother conceded the threshold, but contended that the child should be returned to her care either under a **supervision order** or an interim care order. The ground of appeal was that the judge had failed to carry out a balancing exercise to identify the risks of separating the child from the mother with the risk of returning home.

The Court of Appeal probes very carefully an important aspect of the judicial decision making – the welfare checklist.

The guidance that has emerged gives members of the judiciary a clear direction on what needs to be considered.

1 The court must establish the facts and, in particular, it must make findings on any relevant facts or disputed facts.
2 The court must then evaluate whether, on the basis of these facts, the s. 31 CA89 threshold is crossed.
3 The court should then apply the welfare checklist to the circumstances of the case.
4 If the case involves a plan of adoption, the court should also apply the welfare checklist as set out in the Adoption and Children Act 2002 to the circumstances of the case.
5 The court should then consider proportionately when determining what order to make, and in an adoption case it must specifically address the formulation set down by the Supreme Court in *Re B* [2013] in essence that '*nothing else will do*'.

The welfare checklist will be considered in more detail in Chapter 2, but it is important to highlight from the onset the importance of this principle; both historically and in our current child protection law and practice. The welfare principle is defined in s. 1(1):

1

(1) When a court determines any question with respect to—
   (a) the upbringing of a child; or
   (b) the administration of a child's property or the application of any income arising from it, the child's welfare shall be the court's paramount consideration.

CA89

In order for the court to address this important issue, social workers will be required to evidence knowledge of the needs, wishes and feelings of each child in considerable detail as this should form the basis of every **assessment**. Furthermore, the welfare checklist should be used to decide whether or not it is in the child's best interest to make an application to court and for what order, and this will require an assessment of risk.

The current child protection system

In a climate of austerity, timescales and targets, the question needs to be considered as to whether children and their families matter sufficiently within the current child protection system in England. Achieving effective **partnership**-working in the context of child protection has become increasingly elusive, particularly when parents are notified that the local authority is considering compulsory intervention to remove their children under the CA89 (Broadhurst and Holt, 2010). Moreover, recent changes to legislation, policy and practice ushered in with the aim of achieving earlier decisions within the timeframe for the child are indeed laudable, but there are consequences for both children and their parents. The aspirations of achieving case resolution prior to proceedings contained within both the original *Public Law Outline* (*PLO*) (Ministry of Justice (MoJ), 2008) and the recent Practice Direction 36C (2013) are well rehearsed, but these changes being introduced with the recent reform of the family justice system, alongside particular constructions of parenting, may be failing to recognize the potential of many parents, if offered appropriate support, to care safely for their children.

The child protection system relies upon the skill and judgment of those individuals who are working with complex family situations. Assessing risk and making decisions in complex situations requires not only the individual attributes above, but also support and resources from both the individual agency and the courts. There are consequences that flow from every decision that is made in respect of a child where there are child protection concerns – these are life changing. The risk of **harm** if the child remains in the home always has to be balanced with the risks if the child is removed.

Achieving unnoticed success in child protection practice paradoxically requires critical, analytical and reflective thinking which informs a clear and thoughtful plan for each child. Knowledge of the law, policies and procedures is crucial in this area of social work practice to ensure families receive a service which is both equitable and respectful when they turn to a system in times of great stress.

Aims of the book

This book aims to provide an understanding of child protection law and practice within a changing political landscape. The Children and Families Bill and the Crime and Courts Bill are currently progressing through Parliament. These will introduce a number of changes not least the creation of a single family court, which was first recommended nearly 40 years ago. The modernization agenda of the Family Court is now set in train and it is expected that all public law child care cases will be concluded within 26 weeks. These challenges will undoubtedly impact on professionals working within the child protection sytem and families who are in receipt of services. This book will focus on the legislation, policies, procedures and protocols which have become so important in this area of practice. Child care law is in the process of revolutionary change, but the task of protecting children relies on the knowledge, skill, competence and confidence of key professionals who are tasked with protecting the most vulnerable children in our society. It is a vitally important area of practice that is both highly rewarding and challenging in equal measures.

Outline of chapters

Chapter 1 explores the key principles of the Children Act and examines in some depth the welfare principle and how important this is when making decisions about a child. The duty to investigate when a child is suffering or likely to suffer **significant harm** is considered and importantly there is a focus from the onset as to the importance of keeping the child at the heart of the child protection system.

Chapter 2 probes the complex area of decision making, assessment and working with others. The role of the **Local Safeguarding Children Board** (LSCB) is explained and some key messages from the author's experience of **serious case reviews** (SCRs) are shared.

The decision whether to apply for an emergency protection order (EPO), seek police protection or use alternative ways to deal with an emergency will follow an assessment of risk. Chapter 3 explores the law and case law in respect of **emergency applications** and the local authority response when a child who lives or is found in the area is suffering or likely to suffer significant harm and what action should/could be taken to ensure that the welfare of the child is protected.

Chapter 4 on care and supervision orders provides a detailed examination of the law and practice in relation to the application for a care or supervision order. The important issues of **contact** and care planning are also covered here.

Chapter 5 'Policies, procedures and protocols: a way forward post-Munro' examines in some detail the growth of policies and procedures and the impact of change for practitioners. The key message here is, notwithstanding the pressure to achieve targets and timescales, the priority must be on good practice and ultimately the most approproate outcome for the child.

Chapter 6 'Preparing to go to court' provides practical assistance for practitioners who are not familiar with giving evidence in court and examines the roles of other professionals such as the Children and Family Court Advisory and Support Service (Cafcass). The key to navigating this complex area of practice without too much difficulty is the need for good preparation, and advice is given on how to start this ahead of being required to go to court.

Finally, Chapter 7 considers the current developments witin the family justice system that will lead to a single family court in 2014. There is revolutionary change taking place within the family justice system that will have an impact for all professionals working within it. There are challenges for practitioners but also opportunities for working together to ensure children remain at the heart of the child protection system.

1
CHILD CARE LAW AND PRACTICE

The Children Act 1989

The CA89 is arguably the most innovative, comprehensive and far-reaching reform of child law that has ever been enacted. It is a comprehensive piece of legislation that consolidates and integrates almost all the preceding legislation relating to children. The Act integrated public and private law provisions for the first time and removed the link with criminal law for young people (s. 90(1) CA89). This was subsequently changed with the introduction of s. 12(7) Crime and Disorder Act 1998 which creates a different route into care in respect of a child under the age of ten who has committed an act that, had they been aged ten or over, would have constituted an offence, or where there has been a failure to comply with any requirements made under a child safety order (s. 11 Crime and Disorder Act 1998; s. 60 Children Act 2004 (CA04)).

Furthermore, the CA89 has been described as 'consensus legislation' and followed a series of influential reports regarding the intervention of local authorities in the 1980s to protect children. Three significant and important public inquiries following child deaths (notably Jasmine Beckford (1985), Tyra Henry (1985) and Kimberley Carlile (1987); see respectively Blom-Cooper et al., 1985; Arnold, 1987; Harding et al., 1987) highlighted the failure of safeguarding agencies to work together successfully to protect children and the failure of local authorities to intervene, particularly when parents were hard to reach. These reports were paralleled by the Cleveland Report where local authorities and health professionals were criticized for over-zealous diagnosis of sexual abuse and too hasty intervention that overrode the rights of parents (Butler-Sloss, 1988).

Moreover, the CA89 in this context was broadly welcomed as legislation aimed at reducing the intervention of the state in family life and, certainly, the guiding principle of the Act is the belief that parents are responsible for looking after their children. However, it also includes stronger and clearer duties to investigate when a child '*has suffered*' or '*is likely to suffer significant harm*'. The Act introduced the concept of '*likelihood*' into the threshold for care and supervision orders, which will be explained further below.

Key principles of the Children Act 1989

The CA89 enshrined a number of guiding principles. These principles are nothing more than good practice, but it made explicit the value base for interpreting and applying the law.

Welfare of the child

1

(1) When a court determines any question with respect to—
   (a) the upbringing of a child; or
   (b) the administration of a child's property or the application of any income arising from it, the child's welfare shall be the court's paramount consideration.

CA89

Furthermore, s. 1(4) CA89 states that:

1

(3) a court shall have regard in particular to—
   (a) the ascertainable wishes and feelings of the child concerned (considered in the light of his age and understanding);
   (b) his physical, emotional and educational needs;
   (c) the likely effect on him of any change in his circumstances;
   (d) his age, sex, background and any characteristics of his which the court considers relevant;
   (e) any harm which he has suffered or is at risk of suffering;
   (f) how capable each of his parents, and any other person in relation to whom the court considers the question to be relevant, is of meeting his needs;
   (g) the range of powers available to the court under this Act in the proceedings in question.

CA89

The welfare of a child must be the paramount consideration of both the court and practitioners working within the child protection system. In any decision about the care of a child, it is the child's welfare that must remain the focus. It is all too easy to focus on the needs and competing agendas of the adults within the family and assume from assessments with the parents that the needs and wishes of the child are understood. Practitioners tasked with representing children must be able to address the questions raised in the welfare checklist and consider whether they have detailed knowledge of the child sufficient to be able to address the checklist and identify the needs, wishes and feelings of the child. Effective communication and engagement with children is crucial in child protection work and this should always remain the focus and priority (Lefevre, 2010).

Furthermore, practitioners need to be able to provide a detailed assessment of each element of the checklist and importantly be in a position to provide a critically reflective and analytical assessment to inform the care plan. The welfare checklist must be considered in any application to the court for a care or supervision order and where an application under s. 8 CA89 is contested. It is the author's view that best practice should involve the welfare checklist being considered in every case where there are child protection concerns. It is imperative when undertaking an assessment of risk to agree both a plan and a contingency plan and, to achieve this aim, consideration of the welfare checklist is strongly advised.

Moreover, the court must ascertain the wishes and feelings of the child and will not make an Order unless this is *'better for the child than making no order at all'* (s. 1(5) CA89).

On-the-spot questions

1 Should practitioners use the welfare checklist when making decisions about any child, regardless of whether an application is being made to court or not?

2 If the welfare checklist is not considered in every case, how do you determine when an application should or should not be made and what alternative decisions could/should be made in respect of the child?

Threshold criteria

It is a contentious issue that to remove a child from his or her family requires the applicant local authority to satisfy the court only on the balance of probabilities that the child *'has suffered, or is likely to suffer, significant harm'* (s. 31(2) CA89).

31

(2) A court may only make a care order or supervision order if it is satisfied—
  (a) that the child concerned is suffering, or is likely to suffer, significant harm; and

(b) that the harm, or likelihood of harm, is attributable to—
    (i) the care given to the child, or likely to be given to him if the order were not made, not being what it would be reasonable to expect a parent to give to him; or
    (ii) the child's being beyond parental control.

CA89

In s. 31(9) CA89, 'harm' is defined as *'ill-treatment or the impairment of health or development including, for example, impairment suffered from seeing or hearing the ill-treatment of another'*; *'*ill-treatment*' 'includes sexual abuse and forms of ill-treatment which are not physical'*; 'health' *'means physical or mental health'*; and 'development' *'means physical, intellectual, emotional, social or behavioural development'.*

The **threshold criteria** outlined by Baroness Hale at paras 70 and 72 in *Re B (Care Proceedings: Standard of Proof)* [2008] mean the test which must be satisfied before the court can make either a care or supervision order in favour of the local authority. It is essentially the first hurdle, but if we examine the wording of the threshold criteria above and we apply the evidential burden of proof – *balance of possibilities* – we can see there is considerable margin for discretion.

In order for the threshold criteria to be met, the conditions set out in paras (a) and (b) above must be affirmatively established to the satisfaction of the court. The legal burden of establishing the existence of these conditions rests on the applicant for a care order as applied in the decision in *H and Others (Minors)* [1996]. The standard of proof to be applied when establishing the threshold is the civil standard, i.e. the simple balance of probabilities as applied in *Re B (Minors) (Sexual Abuse: Standard of Proof)* [2008].

No order principle

1

(5) Where a court is considering whether or not to make one or more orders under the Act with respect to a child, it shall not make the order or any of the orders unless it considers that doing so would be better for the child than making no order at all [the **no order principle**].

CA89

Prior to the advent of the CA89, the central government-commissioned *Review of Child Care Law* articulated a growing unease about the way in which parents were dealt with under the law at that time, and argued that

> **KEY CASE ANALYSIS**

Re J (Children) [2012], *Re C and B (Care Order: Future Harm)* [2001] and *Re L (A Child)* [2007]

Significant harm is not defined in the Act, but remains the subject of much debate within case law. *Re J (Children)* [2012], *Re C and B (Care Order: Future Harm)* [2001] and *Re L (A Child)* [2007] are three examples but there are many. *Re J* concerned an appeal of an application for a care order on the basis that the threshold was not met. In previous care proceedings concerning the mother's older child from a different relationship, there had been a finding that she was within a 'pool of possible perpetrators' (along with the father of that child) of causing the death of her first baby. The mother then entered into a new relationship with a man and they had a child together. The family moved to another local authority area. The local authority some four years later became aware of the previous proceedings and issued proceedings in respect of the child of this relationship. The court was invited to find the threshold met solely on the basis of the finding in the earlier proceedings: the second local authority raised no other material concerns about the mother's care for the new child. The issue raised by this case, therefore, was whether such a finding could form the basis of the threshold criteria being met. The circuit judge held that it could not. The local authority appealed.

The above cases highlight the important point that significant is not necessarily the same as serious, but a serious situation could be deemed significant – the local authority will need to provide evidence and satisfy the court that the child has suffered or is likely to suffer *significant* harm. The interim removal of children was discussed in detail in *Re J, Re C and B* and *Re L*. However, a recurrent theme in these cases is that the risk to a child must be imminent and really serious to justify removal. This does not mean the local authority should not make an application for a care order if the threshold criteria are met and the child is suffering or is likely to suffer significant harm, but the decision to remove a child must be justifiable, reasonable and proportionate, and the evidence relied upon by the local authority should be open to challenge and judicial scrutiny.

> ◢ **PRACTICE FOCUS**
>
> Nancy is 34. Following the birth of her son Jasper aged six months, she has been diagnosed with a serious neurological disorder that has resulted in substantial loss of vision and speech, limited mobility and the prognosis of a life expectancy of five years. Nancy has no family; both her parents died when Nancy was in her early twenties and she has no siblings. Prior to becoming pregnant Nancy spent a couple of years using non-prescribed drugs and consuming large quantities of alcohol. It was during this period, when she was travelling and engaging in a number of casual relationships with men, that she became pregnant with Jasper. Nancy is not able to confirm the identity of Jasper's father.
>
> Nancy's health continues to deteriorate and she requires 24/7 care in her own home. Nancy is not able to directly care for Jasper, but is able, when she is motivated to do so, to do this via her own care staff. Nancy spends long periods asleep and her routine involves her usually getting out of bed by 11am and then returning to bed by 7pm. Nancy has reported feeling low in mood and is concerned about the future for Jasper as she is aware of her own prognosis and what this will mean for him.
>
> Jasper is making good progress and he presents as a happy, contented child who is developing very well. Nancy is not able to hold Jasper unaided but manages to cuddle him with the assistance of one of three regular care staff. Jasper responds very well to the care staff who have assisted Nancy with his care since his birth. Children's social care is considering making an application for a care order in respect of Jasper.
>
> What will you need to evidence in terms of the threshold criteria and can you anticipate any difficulties?

parents should be allowed to fulfil their 'natural' and 'legal' responsibilities (Department of Health and Social Security (DHSS) 1985(b) para. 2.8).

Drawing a conclusion that children were best cared for by their families, the review stated that, wherever possible, the state should seek to support rather than usurp the responsibilities of parents. Of course, what is commonly described as the 'Cleveland Crisis' further strengthened a growing impetus towards achieving an effective balance between the powers of the state and the rights and responsibilities of parents (Butler-Sloss, 1988). Although there has been significant debate about the political context and connotations of the concept of parental responsibility within the CA89 (cf. Edwards and Halpern, 1992), there is consensus that the increased range of powers and duties that this Act introduced signified a genuine attempt to ensure parents were supported in the upbringing of their children (Buchanan, 1994; Kaganas et al., 1995; Corby et al., 1996).

Within the detail of the CA89, it is possible to identify a range of measures designed to support **parental responsibility** and partnership practices. In Part 1, s. 3(1) of the Act, the concept of parental responsibility is formally laid out – described by Felicity Kaganas (1995:8) as the 'lynchpin of partnership ideology'. Throughout the Act, the statute supports parental responsibility even when children are subject to intervention from the state. Indeed, under Parts IV and V of the Act, parents retain parental responsibility when children are subject to care and supervision orders, with the local authority obligated to support contact between parents and children living away from home. The Act's aspiration to support the upbringing of children by their parents (wherever possible) is particularly clear in the no order/least restrictive order s. 1(5) principle – which, as discussed, is now reinforced through the *PLO* (2008), which will be dealt with in detail in Chapter 6.

Parental responsibility

Furthermore, the Act introduced the concept of parental responsibility, defined as *'all the rights, duties, powers, responsibilities and authority which by law a parent of a child has in relation to the child and his property'* (s. 3(1) CA89). Parental responsibility is awarded in respect of birth status and residence arrangements. The birth mother automatically has parental responsibility and retains it irrespective of whether the child remains living with her or not until the child reaches 16. The birth father has parental responsibility if at the time of the child's birth he was married to the mother, or if he subsequently marries the mother. The birth father also has parental responsibility if (after 1 December 2003) he registers the child's birth jointly with the mother. If none of the above apply, the birth father may have parental responsibility if he and the child's mother make a parental responsibility agreement; or if he applies to the court and the court grants permission. Other people – e.g. a stepfather or stepmother or grandparent – can acquire parental responsibility on the making of an adoption order, residence order, or guardianship. Any person for whom a residence order is made in respect of a particular child holds parental responsibility for the duration of the order; or, if they are a parent of the child, they retain it even after the order is discharged.

The local authority obtains parental responsibility when a care order is in force, but parental responsibility is shared with the birth parents. This requires the local authority as a corporate parent to consult with the parents with regards to any important decisions with respect to the child, as would be reasonable to expect any parents to do.

Once parental responsibility has been given to a birth father (if he is not automatically entitled through marriage), he cannot have it removed from him even if the child does not live with him. In *Re S (Parental Responsibility)* [1995], it was stated by Lord Justice Ward that in separated families the child needs to have a positive image of the parent he no longer lives with in order to bolster his own self-esteem.

The birth father has precedence over others in relation to guardianship of children after the death of the birth mother; however, if there is a residence order in force in someone else's name when the mother dies, that person also has parental responsibility as long as the residence order is in force (Hester et al., 2006)

> **On-the-spot question**
>
> How do you ensure you have consulted and involved all who hold parental responsibility in respect of the child, including men?

Partnership

In order to carry out the duties as a corporate parent as discussed above, achieving good levels of communication between those who hold parental responsibility for the child is pivotal. Working in partnership is a central principle of the Act, but achieving good partnership working in the context of child protection requires skill, good judgment and commitment. Central to achieving good partnership working is the requirement to consider rights, duties, responsibilities and communication. These terms are vague and open to varying degrees of interpretation and application (Kaganas, 1995).

The term 'partnership working' has been probed consistently since the late 1980s in a number of important studies, inquiry reports and government-commissioned reviews (DHSS, 1985a; De'Ath and Pugh,

1985–86; Pugh et al., 1987; Butler-Sloss, 1988; Aldgate, 1989) paving the way for what we now consider to be a central and guiding principle for effective social work practice with children and families – that is partnership working. Citing the benefits of effective parental engagement for the welfare of children, studies drew attention to the **human rights** issues with respect to state intervention within the family (Pugh and De'Ath, 1985; Milham et al., 1986). In particular, increasing calls for a greater degree of power-sharing between professionals and parents were soon to be consolidated in policy and legislation through the advent of the CA89 and associated volumes of regulations and guidance. Whilst the word 'partnership' did not appear in the Act, the 1989 Department of Health (DoH) guidance document, *The Care of Children: Principles and Practice in Regulations and Guidance*, published prior to the Act's implementation, made very clear its underpinning ethos and aspirations.

Despite the positive legislation of the CA89, a raft of studies has identified the problems of translating the ideals of partnership into practice realities (Buchanan, 1994; DoH, 1995; Thoburn et al., 1995; Woodhouse, 1995; Corby et al., 1996; Freeman and Hunt, 1998; Holland and Scourfield, 2004; Brophy, 2006; Harlow and Shardlow, 2006). Indeed, since the implementation of the CA89, and contrary to the intents and ethos of the Act, a very significant rise in applications made to the courts under s. 31 CA89 has been evident (Holt et al., 2013). Study after study has found that the pursuit of consensual solutions in the context of child protection can prove particularly elusive (Nelken, 1987; Aldgate, 1989; Buchanan, 1994; Kaganas et al., 1995; Corby et al., 1996; Hunt et al., 1999; Harlow and Shardlow, 2006; Masson et al., 2008) (all cited in Broadhurst and Holt, 2010:99).

Under the revised CA89 guidance (Department for Children, Schools and Families (DCSF), 2008), a range of professionals is implicated in partnership work with parents; however, the case-holding local authority social worker will continue to be a key player in promoting parental engagement. As is discussed in the following sections, whilst the concept of partnership working has a long history, the difficulties of establishing partnerships with parents appear to endure.

The level of conflict between parents and the state stems from discordance between parents' views of the causes for concern and those of the state, as well as disagreement about the need for compulsory removal of children (Harwin, 1992; Freeman and Hunt, 1998; Brophy, 2006). Freeman and Hunt (1998) found that there was little agreement between parents and professionals about the grounds for concern and parents were extremely negative about the help offered from the local authority.

Studies have found that parents struggle to make sense of the court process; whilst attempts may be made to offer explanations to parents, processes can confuse and alienate. Appearing in court can be stressful for all parties, but as Freeman and Hunt's (1998) study highlighted, parents can experience stress even outside of the courtroom. For parents, simply waiting to enter court can be difficult on account of the lack of privacy coupled with a sense of anxiety and shame (Lindley, 1994a). Research has also found that parents can perceive their statements as inconsequential when weighted against those of professionals (Brophy, 2006). Of course, the conversion rates of local authority applications to the granting of orders by the courts appear to bear this out (cf. Welbourne, 2008, for a fuller discussion). Parents are only too aware of the contradictions within law and practice and that their rights as parents can be significantly curtailed where allegations of significant harm are made (Farmer and Owen, 1995).

On-the-spot question	What are the benefits and difficulties of partnership working?

Children in need/child protection: where is the boundary?

17

(1) It shall be the general duty of every local authority to (a) to safeguard and promote the welfare of children within their area who are in need; and (b) so far as is consistent with that duty, to promote the upbringing of such children by their families, by providing a range and level of services appropriate to those children's needs.

CA89

The duty applies only to children who are defined as in need under the CA89. In law a child shall be taken to be in need if:

17(10)

(a) he is unlikely to achieve or maintain, or to have the opportunity of achieving or maintaining, a reasonable standard of health or development without the provision for him of services by a local authority under this Part;

(b) his health or development is likely to be significantly impaired or
    further impaired, without the provision for him of such services; or
(c) he is disabled.

CA89

Reasonable standard and significantly impaired are not defined in the
Act; the intention of Parliament was to leave these important terms to be
negotiated in each individual case. However, what constitutes a '*reasonable standard*' of health or development and the likelihood of '*significant*'
or further impairment without the provision of services are crucial in
determining eligibility. It is imperative that the social worker, in consultation with other professionals, provides a deep critical, analytical and
reflective assessment of the child's needs.

There is a specific duty outlined in schedule 2 CA89 para. 6 to provide
services to '*minimise the effect on disabled children ... of their disabilities*'
and '*to give such children the opportunity to lead lives which are as normal
as possible*'.

The local authority is required (s. 17(5) CA89) *to 'secure the required
services, and this may be delegated to other agencies'*. Local authorities have
a statutory duty, to be found in s. 10 CA04, to cooperate with other agencies to ensure the well-being of children and, in the event that an authority whose help is requested as part of the assessment and the assistance is
not forthcoming, may make a formal request for assistance (s. 27 CA89).

The CA89 in s. 17 imposes a general duty to **children in need** and
not specific children. The implications of the wording of the Act mean
that families are not able to take action against a local authority if they
fail to provide services, as evidenced in *R (On the Application of G) (FC) v
London Borough of Southwark* [2009], except that they may seek judicial
review of the decision. An action for judicial review focuses on the procedural aspects of the case and determines whether the local authority has
acted lawfully, reasonably and rationally and properly consulted the
family during the process. The court has a range of powers which can
result in the court making an order quashing the original decision and
inviting the local authority to reconsider the matter. In *Re T (Judicial
Review: Local Authority Decisions Concerning a Child in Need)* (2004) the
court found the process of assessment and decision-making both irrational and unreasonable and quashed the decision.

The boundary between s. 17 in respect of a child in need and s. 47 –
which imposes a duty on the local authority to investigate when it has

concerns that a child in the area is at risk of, or has suffered significant harm – is often conflated. If we consider the case of *Re T* above, children can be '*in need*' as a result of abuse. The outcome of a s. 47 investigation may be to register the child as a child in need and to provide a range of services to the child/family under s. 17 CA89.

Similarly, children with disabilities are by virtue of their disability more vulnerable to abuse. Assessments of children with disabilities where there are concerns about the child's welfare must be undertaken by a range of professionals with expertise in both child protection and disability. The focus of the assessment must be on an understanding of the child's needs and wishes, to avoid over-focusing on the demands upon parents of caring for a child with complex needs. This is clearly an important issue and should not be overlooked, but it must remain in the context of an overall assessment of the child.

Duty to investigate

The CA89 sets out in detail what local authorities and the courts should do to protect the welfare of children. It charges local authorities with the '*duty to investigate ... if they have reasonable cause to suspect that a child who lives, or is found, in their area is suffering, or is likely to suffer, significant harm*' (s. 47 CA89). Local authorities are also charged with a duty to provide '*services for children in need, their families and others*' (s. 17 CA89).

Section 31 CA89 defines 'harm' as '*ill-treatment (including sexual abuse and non-physical forms of ill-treatment) or the impairment of health (physical or mental) or development (physical, intellectual, emotional, social or behavioural)*'. Significant is not defined in the Act, although it does say that the court should compare the health and development of the child '*with that which could be reasonably expected of a similar child*' (s. 31(10) CA89). So the courts have to decide for themselves what constitutes significant harm by looking at the facts of each individual case.

A s. 47 enquiry is initiated to decide whether and what type of action is required to safeguard and promote the welfare of the child who is suspected of or likely to be suffering significant harm. The enquiry is carried out by undertaking an assessment, which analyses the needs of a child and the capacity of the child's parents or caregivers to respond to these needs within the context of their wider family and community.

Local authority social workers have a statutory duty to lead assessments under s. 47 CA89. The police, health professionals, teachers and other relevant professionals must help the local authority in undertaking its enquiries (s. 10 CA04). Furthermore, there is a duty on a range of organizations and individuals to ensure their functions, and any services they contract out to others, are discharged having regard to the need to safeguard and promote the welfare of children (s. 11 CA04).

Two key guidance documents were introduced to help professionals identify children at risk and to work together to protect them: guidance on interagency cooperation under the CA89 was first published in 1991 (Home Office, 1991). *Working Together to Safeguard Children: A Guide to Inter-agency Working to Safeguard and Promote the Welfare of Children* (DCSF, 2010) provided definitions of child abuse and neglect and guidance on what action agencies must take to protect children. Information was provided in relation to roles and responsibilities, the role of LSCBs (which will be discussed more fully in Chapter 2) and SCRs (conducted after the death or serious injury of a child). A revised version of *Working Together to Safeguard Children* was published on 21 March 2013 and came into effect on 15 April 2013 (Department for Education (DfE), 2013). The guidance outlines how organizations and individuals should work together to safeguard and promote the welfare of children and how practitioners should conduct the assessment of children.

This guidance replaces *Working Together to Safeguard Children* (DCSF, 2010); *Framework for the Assessment of Children in Need and their Families* (DoH, 2000); and statutory guidance on making arrangements to safeguard and promote the welfare of children under s. 11 CA04 (2007). The revised document is reduced in size, with a focus on the central issues and legal rules which underpin the safeguarding responsibilities of professionals and organizations. Pivotal in the guidance is the focus on the child's needs which are paramount (para. 6), and should be prioritized at the earliest opportunity to reduce risk and prevent a problem from escalating (para. 4). Importantly, in achieving the above there is a need for professionals to share relevant information in an appropriate and timely manner using expert professional judgment to place the child's needs centrally, so that decision-making and planning is focused on safeguarding and promoting the needs of each individual child. Furthermore, the guidance highlights the importance of regularly reviewing outcomes against the individual plan for each child.

These changes introduced by *Working Together* (DfE, 2013) are in line with the recommendations of the Munro Report, 2011, to remove the prescription of timescales and the distinction between core and initial assessments. Whilst local authorities have a mandatory duty to investigate if they are informed that a child may be at risk, in accordance with legislation and guidance, there are no specific mandatory child abuse reporting laws in the UK that require professionals to report their suspicions to the authorities. However, in Northern Ireland, it is an offence not to report an arrestable crime to the police, which by definition includes most crimes against children (Wallace and Bunting, 2007).

Working Together (DfE, 2013:8) also requires that effective safeguarding arrangements in every local area should be underpinned by two key principles:

1 Safeguarding is everyone's responsibility: for services to be effective each professional and organization should play their full part.
2 A child-centred approach: for services to be effective they should be based on a clear understanding of the needs and views of children.

On-the-spot question	In practice what does 'safeguarding is everyone's responsibility' mean for you?

Delay

1(2)

> In any proceedings in which any question with respect to the upbringing of a child arises, the court shall have regard to the general principle that any **delay** in determining the question is likely to prejudice the welfare of the child.
>
> *CA89*

As part of an ongoing review of policy and practice in safeguarding children in the UK and as a response to the inquiries into child deaths or SCRs in the 1990s and post-2000, a number of important policy, legislative and procedural changes have been introduced: *Care Matters: Time for Change* (Department for Education and Skills (DfES), 2007), the Children and Young Persons Act 2008 and the *PLO* (MoJ, 2008). These changes are intended to optimize outcomes for children and families by reducing delay in the conduct and resolution of cases and by ensuring that costs and resources are effectively managed at all stages of a child protection case. The publication of the *Family Justice Review: Final Report* in 2011

(MoJ, 2011) and *The Government Response to the Family Justice Review: A System with Children and Families at its Heart* published in 2012 (MoJ and DfE, 2012) provides further evidence of the policy agenda. Therein, perhaps, lies the government's greatest difficulty and an apparent paradox: the reforms envisaged are the widest ranging since the advent of the CA89, but government finances have rarely been so stretched. The proposals will require a delicate balancing act, and it is by no means certain that the aim of reducing costs whilst maintaining children and families as the focus will be achieved.

Following the recommendations of the *Family Justice Review*, the government has proposed legislation (MoJ and DfE, 2012:16, para. 55) to impose a statutory six-month time limit for the completion of care cases (the current average time for a case from start to finish is 55 weeks). Where appropriate, cases should be progressed more quickly, and only in *exceptional* cases where the best interests of the child are served and reasons for further delay are clear may an extension be granted. This is reiterated in the third update on *The Family Justice Modernisation Programme* where Ryder J states:

> The single most important change that I recommend is the creation of standard and exceptional case tracks with guidance in the form of a pathway that describes how some cases can and should be completed within 26 weeks.
>
> *Judiciary of England and Wales, 2012:3*

Whilst the rhetoric of prioritizing the timetable for the child is indeed laudable, it appears there is an over-focus on reducing delay in care cases when what is clearly needed is a commitment to provide greater resources and flexibility throughout the process if the system is to maintain children and families at the heart (Gore, 2012).

Furthermore, the *PLO* (MoJ, 2008) replaced the *Protocol for the Judicial Management of Public Law Child Care Cases* (MoJ, 2003) and required a re-ordering of the way care proceedings are instigated, structured and conducted. The *PLO* is a response to both the *Thematic Review* published by the Judicial Review Team (JRT) (2005) and the *Review of Child Care Proceedings in England and Wales* commissioned by the former Department for Constitutional Affairs (DCA) (2006a). These analytic reviews sought to identify the causes of delay/inefficiencies in child care proceedings and, in identifying a number of exacerbating factors, once again drew attention to the importance of parental engagement in ensuring effective decisions for children:

> It is also clear that children can suffer because parents and families are insufficiently engaged in the process both pre-proceedings and during the progress of the case.
>
> *'Foreword'* to PLO, MOJ, 2008

One of the most pertinent responses to the proposals published by the government is that of the Law Society, which points out that the public funding cuts leading to a reduction in the number of firms offering representation in this field will all add to delay *in any case*. To impose a six-month time limit if and when cases go to court will create a pressure cooker and place the system at risk of exploding. The reality of these cases is that many months are lost in court proceedings due to a lack of court time, inefficiency and poor planning at the outset of proceedings – the failure of local authorities to set up assessments in parallel with initiating proceedings or dealing with immediate and pressing issues of placement, and due to a lack of local authority in-house resources building in further delay to assessments. The government has recognized that:

> The quality and timeliness of social care assessments put to the courts has a crucial bearing on how quickly cases progress. Poor or late assessments can lead to delayed or re-scheduled hearings and can result in courts commissioning evidence-gathering elsewhere.
>
> *MoJ and DfE, 2012:14, para. 45*

The hegemonic concern with the timetable for the child reinforces that children 'cannot wait' for parents to change, particularly where parental problems are deemed to be entrenched (Holt et al., 2013).

The rights of the child

On 16 December 1991, the UK government ratified the **United Nations Convention on the Rights of the Child 1989** (UNCRC). It includes the right of the child to: protection from abuse; to express their own views and have them listened to; and to care and services for children with a disability or children living away from home. Although the government has pronounced that it regards itself bound by the Convention and makes reference to it in child protection guidance, it has not become part of UK legislation (Lyon, 2003:2).

Significantly, Wales has enshrined the principles of the UN Convention with a legislative mandate. The National Assembly for Wales passed the Rights of Children and Young Persons (Wales) Measure on 18 January 2011. The measure imposes a legal duty on Welsh ministers to have due regard to the rights and obligations set out in the Convention in exercising any of their functions. There are two stages of the legislation coming into force; from May 2012 it has applied to new or revised legislation or policy and from May 2014 it will apply to all Welsh ministers' functions along with a duty to promote knowledge and understanding of the Convention.

The Children's Commissioner for Wales Act 2001 created the first children's commissioner in the UK. The principal aim of the commissioner is to safeguard and promote the rights and welfare of children. Subsequent legislation created a children's commissioner for Northern Ireland (Commissioner for Children and Young People (NI) Order 2003), Scotland (Commissioner for Children and Young People (Scotland) Act 2003) and England (ss 1–9 CA04).

The English Commissioner is unique in the UK in not having the remit to promote children's rights. It is the Children's Rights Director for England who has independent statutory duties to ascertain and report the views of children living away from home or in care, to advise on children's rights and welfare, and to raise matters which are significant to the rights or welfare of children in England. An independent review of these arrangements was commissioned by the government in 2010; the review's recommendations which have been accepted by the government propose the replacement of the current Children's Commissioner and Children's Rights Director by a new Office of the Children's Commissioner for England, based on new legislation.

Human rights

The European Convention on Human Rights (ECHR) is an international treaty, which was signed by the UK in 1948. The Labour Party introduced a policy paper, *Bringing Rights Home* in 1996 (Klug, 2007) which was incorporated into the Labour Party manifesto and, not without a contest, the ECHR was incorporated into UK legislation with the Human Rights Act 1998.

The passing of this legislation has been hugely influential as individuals are now able to seek remedies from the European Court of Human Rights (ECtHR) in Strasbourg and cases dealt with by the ECtHR are reported in the following way. Applications to the ECtHR are made by individuals against decisions made within the UK courts. Decisions made by the ECtHR are required to be considered by the UK courts and in recent years we have seen UK courts making reference to decisions made in the ECtHR (*Re L (Care Proceedings: Human Rights Claims)* [2003]). Whilst the Human Rights Act 1998 does not specifically mention children's rights, children are covered by legislation as they are persons in the eyes of the law, just as adults are (Bainham, 2005:82).

The Act makes it unlawful for public authorities to act in a manner that is incompatible with the rights and freedoms contained in the Act. It also requires the government and the courts to ensure that court rulings and new Bills are compatible with the Act wherever possible. These rights include the right to respect for private and family life.

Moreover, where important decisions are being made without judicial scrutiny the need to ensure the rights of children and families are upheld in accordance with the ECHR 1951 is crucial. Article 8 ECHR must apply equally to decision-making outside of the court in exactly the same way as decisions made within court proceedings, as found in *Re B (Care: Interference with Family Life)* [2003]. In child protection cases Article 8 guarantees fairness in the decision-making process and the procedural safeguards mandated by Article 8 should apply equally and not be compromised by rhetoric which implies placing children at the heart of the system, or by imposing guidance which suggests otherwise.

There are inevitably cases where decision-making by a local authority has been challenged within the judiciary. For example, the ECtHR on 16 March 2010 in *AD and OD v UK* ruled that the failure by a local authority to conduct a risk assessment resulting in a child being placed with foster parents was a breach of Article 8.

In *R (L and Others) v Manchester City Council* [2001], Manchester City Council's policy on payments to kinship carers was successfully challenged as a result of the local authority adopting a policy of paying less to relative foster carers. This effectively prevented the continuation of a family placement and as a result the rights of the child under Article 8 were not respected. The action was taken against the local authority as a result of the decision made at the pre-proceedings stage to pay short-term kinship carers of looked after children significantly less than approved local authority foster carers. Once approved as long-term carers, they were paid at the normal rate.

Munby J found the local authority policy to be both irrational and contrary to Article 8 ECHR. The impact of the judgment is that payments to kinship carers must be made on the same basis as local authority carers whether it is a short-term or long-term arrangement. Any difference should relate to the child's needs, the skills of the carer, or some other relevant factor that is used as a basis for an authority-wide policy. In another matter Munby J was concerned with the fairness of local authority decision-making after a care order had been made. Parents complained that the local authority had, in effect, substituted an entirely new care plan involving removal of their children without including them properly in the process. In *Re D (Minor) (Care or Supervision Order)* [1993] it was noted that an authority should not alter such plans without due consultation with the family, applied in the case of *Re G (Care: Challenge to the Local Authority's Decision)* [2003]. It is now accepted beyond doubt that both parents and children are persons under the ECHR and that children, too, possess 'Convention rights'. Along with parents, children are afforded exactly the same procedural guarantees, protection and fairness mandated by Article 8 as highlighted in *Re S (FC) (A Child)* [2004].

Childcare law remains dominated by the concept that the child's welfare is paramount. In *Re KD (A Minor) (Ward: Termination of Access)* [1988], Lord Oliver found there to be no conflict in the tension between the paramountcy principle and the Convention. However, there are a number of less desirable consequences in practice. Significantly, the focus on the child's welfare tends to divert attention away from the child's rights (Featherstone et al., 2010). Consistently evidenced in child death inquiry reports and SCRs, the child's right to participate meaningfully in the decision-making process and his or her right to be heard are often not afforded due significance (Brandon et al., 2009).

In child protection practice it can be seen that the ECHR requires the state to engage in a most sensitive balancing exercise. The incorporation of the Convention has implications for the way in which local authorities and the courts conduct themselves in performing their statutory role and, in respect of the local authority, for the allocation of resources. Once again the boundary of decision-making is pertinent. This balancing exercise was highlighted in *Re KD* [1988] where the court reaffirmed that parents should not expect to be granted additional assessments on the

> **PRACTICE FOCUS**
>
> Returning to the case study of Jasper and Nancy (see page 13). The local authority is considering resource allocation and the issue has been raised in relation to the cost of supporting both Jasper and Nancy in their own home. The budget is currently shared between children's social care and adults, but the pressure is on to reduce this spend in the current climate of austerity. The social worker and manager have been asked to consider making an application for a care order with a view to seeking a permanent placement for Jasper outside of the home. As the social worker for Jasper, you want to argue a strong case for Jasper remaining at home with his mother. How do Lord Oliver's comments in *Re KD* and the ECHR assist you in presenting a convincing argument to the local authority? What issues might you face if you were to make an application to court?

basis that they should be given every reasonable opportunity to put forward a positive case. The judge hearing the individual case is surely best placed to decide whether an assessment is necessary in order to provide the court with the best possible evidence, as opposed to causing an unnecessary delay and giving parents too much latitude. However, central to the system is the need to ensure rigour and scrutiny in the most difficult decisions.

Current policy and practice

The death of Victoria Climbié in 2000 resulted in a government inquiry led by Lord Laming to consider whether the current legislation was sufficiently robust or whether new legislation was required to improve the child protection system in England. The government's response to the Victoria Climbié inquiry report (DoH, 2003) was the *Keeping Children Safe* report (DfES, 2003b) and the *Every Child Matters* Green Paper (DfES, 2003a), which in turn led to the CA04.

The CA04 establishes the framework and process for integrating services to children. In addition to establishing the post of Children's Commissioner for England, the CA04 places a duty on local authorities to appoint a director of children's services and an elected lead member for children's services, who is responsible for the delivery of services.

The Act places a duty on local authorities and their partners (including the police, health service providers and the youth justice system) to cooperate in promoting the well-being of children and young people and to make arrangements to safeguard and promote the welfare of children. The Act also puts LSCBs on a statutory footing (replacing the non-statutory Area Child Protection Committees) and gives them functions of investigation and review (s. 14), which will be considered further in Chapter 2.

Section 58 CA04 further amends the legislation on physical punishment. It restricts the use of the defence of reasonable punishment so that it can no longer be used when individuals are charged with the offences against a child of wounding, actual or grievous bodily harm or cruelty. Therefore any injury sustained by a child that is serious enough to warrant a charge of assault occasioning actual bodily harm cannot be considered to be as the result of reasonable punishment (DCSF, 2007).

The tragic death of baby Peter Connelly in August 2007 resulted in the government seeking a further inquiry, again led by Lord Laming, in 2009 (House of Commons, 2009). Lord Laming made in total 58 recommendations. Lord Laming's review of children's services in England concluded that child protection issues in England had not had 'the priority they deserved' and many of the reforms brought in after Victoria Climbié's death in 2000 had not been properly implemented.

Other findings included that: there had been an 'over-emphasis on process and targets', resulting in a 'loss of confidence' among social workers, who were overstretched and insufficiently trained; progress was being 'hampered' by the lack of a centralized computer system and an 'over-complicated ... tick-box assessment and recording system'; there was a lack of communication and joined-up working between agencies; and a lack of funding made social work and child protection work a 'Cinderella service' – the sentiments expressed by Lord Laming have been more recently echoed by commentators such as Broadhurst et al. (2011) and Professor Eileen Munro in her review of child protection published in May 2011 which will be discussed further below.

In June 2010 the Coalition government invited Professor Eileen Munro to conduct an independent review of children's social work and child protection practice in England. The first report of the Munro Review of Child Protection (*Part One: A Systems Analysis*) confirmed a number of key themes from the critiques that emerged in the aftermath of the tragic death of baby Peter Connelly. In particular, the report raises concerns about the negative impact of inspection and performance management regimes on the priorities of frontline workers. Munro (2010:7) describes the excessive technical emphasis of recent reforms to social work – 'increasing rules, more detailed procedures and more use of ICT' that have reduced the time available for direct *engagement* with families. In a call to reclaim professional judgment, the review suggests that social workers' dependence on prescriptive rules should be replaced by 'best professional principles' and 'guided judgement' (Munro, 2010:31). Munro notes that a more effective model of practice requires *interaction* with children and their families backed up by good quality reflective supervision (Featherstone et al., 2011). The *Munro Review of Child Protection: Final Report: A Child-Centred System* published in May 2011 called for a child-focused system and a reduction in prescriptive timescales and targets from central government. *A Child-Centred System: The Government's Response to the Munro Review* (DfE, 2011) accepted all but one of Munro's recommendations, and laid out a programme of proposed changes over the following years.

Summary

Child protection work is both rewarding and immensely challenging. It is, however, the area of social work practice where practitioners can feel most exposed – assessments are scrutinized by parents, professionals and the courts, and a mistake can have tragic consequences. The pressure to navigate organizational demands, respond to the needs of children and families, as recommended by both Munro and the Family Justice Review, and achieve timelier decision-making when complex cases go to court are only part of the task of child protection work.

Good child protection work is dependent upon professional, highly skilled and committed practitioners who are competent in producing the detailed risk assessments required to inform good decision-making and planning. Accomplishing good assessments in partnership with parents and extended family are crucial if we are to make the right decisions for children and their families when they turn to a system at times of great stress and when they are in crisis. Ensuring continuing professional development through good supervision and training is crucial in enabling practitioners to keep up to date with their knowledge of the law, policy and practice in this area.

Further reading

Brandon, M and J Thoburn (2008) 'Safeguarding children in the UK: a longitudinal study of services to children suffering or likely to suffer significant harm' 13(4) *Child and Family Social Work* 365–77. Includes further detail from a research study that highlights the services provided to children where there are child protection concerns.

Broadhurst, K and K E Holt (2010) 'Partnership and the limits of procedure: prospects for relationships between parents and professionals under the new public law outline' 15 *Child and Family Social Work* 97–106. Provides a review of the literature highlighting the tensions in achieving good partnership working in the context of child protection practice.

Holt, K E and N Kelly (2012b) 'Rhetoric and reality surrounding care proceedings: family justice under strain' 34(2) *Journal of Social Welfare and Family Law* 155–66 http://dx.doi.org/10.1080/09649069.2012.718531. Examines the boundary of decision-making within the context of child protection practice and probes the changing context of a move away from judicial decision-making to the administrative space of the pre-proceedings meetings.

2
DECISION-MAKING, ASSESSMENT AND WORKING WITH OTHERS

Social work practice is premised on the discretion and professional judgment of social workers (Munro, 2011). Indeed, the administration of children's social care rests on the basis of decision-making in complex cases. Decisions are based on discretion and judgment – when undertaking assessments, where decisions about resources are being made, or when and where contact between parents and their children should take place and whether this should be supervised or not. In brief, social workers and their managers in a variety of contexts make decisions that significantly affect people's lives. Indeed, in child protection social work, they can lead to the altering of people's status (Swain, 2009).

The rights of children and parents to participate and be represented in decision-making has always been difficult. It is accepted that the aspirations of the policy and legislative mandates to achieving consensual solutions in safeguarding children are laudable, as is the wish to keep the rights of children and parents at the heart of the process, in line with the government's response to the *Family Justice Review* (MoJ, 2011).

The child's voice

In 1991, the UK government ratified the UNCRC. The treaty provides a guarantee of rights to children and young people in the UK, including the right, depending on the age and level of understanding of the child or young person, to express their views and to be listened to.

The importance of keeping the child at the heart of child protection practice must be central to good child protection practice. Learning messages from research into SCRs provides important evidence as to the problems when children do not remain at the heart of the child protection system (Ofsted, 2011). Social workers must reclaim their skills in working with children and be in a position to know both the detail and to be able to analyse the needs, wishes and feelings of the child from direct knowledge and not upon a reliance on third-party information. Pivotal, is the need for participation to be a process rather than an event. Listening to and working closely with children has to be based on a sound theoretical understanding, a child-centred philosophy supported with practical skills, good supervision and appropriate and regular training (Freeman, 1992).

> Young people's wishes must be elicited and taken seriously. Even quite young children should be enabled to contribute to decisions about their lives in an age appropriate way. Learning to make a well informed choice is an important aspect of growing up and must involve more than just sitting in on reviews and conferences at which adults have all the power and make decisions.
>
> *DoH, 1990:12*

As a starting point, social workers need to have an understanding of what children are able/not able to do or understand at different ages. Knowledge of child development and an ability to apply this to practice is absolutely pivotal in a social work assessment of a child's development: highlighting delay or regression. In addition, it is crucial to understand age-appropriate play and what concepts/ideas children may comprehend. Vera Fahlberg (1981; 1991) provides consistently clear and helpful guidance in these areas that is not only detailed but also provides a more general likelihood of physical attainment. A working knowledge of attachment theory is essential. Children who are in contact with children's social care are likely to be suffering difficulties around attachment, loss and separation: Aldgate and Simmonds (1988) emphasize that it is almost impossible to understand the impact of separation without a good understanding of attachment theory. Pivotal to understanding how the theory links with practice is direct contact with the child who must always remain at the centre of the system. Resource constraints must never be a reason not to prioritize direct contact with the child in his or her own environment. The importance of meeting with, observing and hearing the child cannot be underestimated, yet all too often this takes a secondary place to organizational demands on practitioner time (Ferguson, 2011).

The final report of Eileen Munro (2011) introduced a series of recommendations, including removing some of the bureaucracy that prevents direct contact with families which local authorities nationally are looking to implement. Whilst it is laudable that these recommendations were made by Munro, it is nevertheless a sad reflection that, within the context of a data surveillance culture within children's social care, there has of late been a preoccupation with data input – controlling and managing rather than facilitating, listening and exploring. Moving frontline workers away from direct contact with children, where these skills are further developed, has led to an erosion of any knowledge/skills social workers gained during their training (Hall et al., 2010; Wastell et al., 2010; White et al., 2010).

In practice social workers should use both their own direct observations of babies and young children and those of other people who know the particular child to make sense of these observations in relation to risk factors. Contact with children and young people should be arranged in places that are familiar to them but there is also an important need to see children and young people away from their carers where it is appropriate to do so. The wishes and feelings of children must be recorded. It is crucially important that the needs of disabled children are identified and this includes needs relating to protection.

On-the-spot question	How do we ensure that we keep children at the heart of the child protection system?

Referrals

The local authority's role to support children and their families is enshrined in Part III of the CA89. Whilst the focus of children's social care may appear to be child protection, it is preventative work that should be attempted in the first instance and only when the family and services fail to protect children should child protection procedures be invoked.

Schedule 2 CA89 outlines the local authority's preventative duty. The local authority must take reasonable steps to:

- prevent children suffering ill treatment and neglect (schedule 2, para. 4);
- reduce the need for care proceedings or criminal proceedings against children (schedule 2, para. 7(a)(i) and (ii));
- avoid the need to place children in secure accommodation (schedule 2, para. 7(c));
- discourage children in their area from committing criminal offences (schedule 2, para. 7 (b)).

The broad scope of schedule 2 has resulted in a practice approach driven by financial constraints and the criteria of eligibility have been tightened in order to protect the budget for child protection. Crucially important at the referral stage is to determine whether this is a child in need or a child protection matter or both.

Referral into children's social care

Anyone who has concerns about a child's welfare can make a referral to local authority children's social care. Referrals can be made by the child themselves, professionals such as teachers, the police and health visitors, as well as family members and members of the public. Initially children's social care has the responsibility to clarify with the referrer the nature and context of the concerns.

When professionals make a referral to children's social care they must include all information they have on the child's developmental needs and the capacity of the child's parents to meet these within the context of the wider family and environment.

The referrer must always have the opportunity to discuss his or her concerns with a qualified social worker (DCSF, 2010, para. 5.32). In some local authorities it is the practice to adopt a 'one-stop shop' for all referrals regardless of their nature, resulting in delay and in some situations a misunderstanding of the presenting issues.

Furthermore, the aspirations, contained within the guidance *Working Together to Safeguard Children* (DfE, 2013) on making arrangements to safeguard and promote the welfare of children under s. 11 CA04 (2007), state that, within one working day of a referral being received, a qualified social worker must make a decision about the course of action to be taken. Moreover, it is anticipated that a qualified social worker will need to make a professional judgment as to what type and level of help and support is needed, record this and feed back to the referrer, the child and his or her family. There will no longer be a requirement to conduct separate initial and core assessments but the maximum timeframe for the assessment to conclude, such that it is possible to reach a decision on the next steps, should be no longer than 45 working days from the point of referral. The assessment may need to be undertaken in a shorter timeframe if the individual needs of the child and the nature and level of risk of harm to the child necessitate this. The guidance requires that local authorities, together with their partners, should develop and publish local protocols for assessment.

Although not made explicit in the guidance, pivotal in achieving timelier decision-making at the referral stage is effective and responsive first-line management.

Response to a referral

Following a referral to children's social care, the local authority is responsible for making an appropriate, timely and proportionate response depending on the child's needs. Furthermore, a decision should be made as to whether the child may be in need and should be assessed under s. 17 CA89. Alternatively, the referral information may suggest the child requires immediate protection and there is reasonable cause to suspect that the child is suffering, or likely to suffer, significant harm and must be assessed under s. 47 CA89. Importantly, the social worker should make an assessment as to what *services* are required by the child and the family and what types of further specialist assessments are required in order to help the local authority to decide what further action to take.

In addition to children's social care, other professionals (for example, housing officers) have a duty to cooperate under s. 27 CA89 by assisting the local authority in carrying out its children's social care functions. Furthermore, the police have a responsibility to carry out investigations into allegations of crimes: the evidence from these may be crucial in an overall assessment of the situation and to inform decision-making.

Where a s. 47 enquiry is being undertaken, the police should work jointly with the local authority. The police and children's social care must coordinate a response following a referral and local protocols approved by LSCBs should be in place to give clear procedures to both agencies on how to work jointly in response to a referral. Children's social care must hold a strategy discussion/meeting whenever there is reasonable cause to suspect that a child has suffered or is likely to suffer significant harm. A strategy discussion can take the form of a telephone conversation or a meeting depending on the urgency and nature of the referral. The purpose of the strategy discussion/meeting is to determine whether a child is in need of immediate protection and for an agency with statutory child protection powers (police, the local authority, the National Society for the Prevention of Cruelty to Children (NSPCC)) to make a decision as to whether emergency action may be necessary to safeguard a child (DoE, 2013:29). The strategy discussion/meeting should take place immediately as there needs to be a decision made on the course of action within one working day of referral followed by a timely assessment based on the needs of the child within 45 working days (DfE, 2013:32).

Assessment of risk

Social workers are required particularly in the context of child protection to deal with a great deal of uncertainty within a context of crisis and stress and this can be overwhelming for the most experienced of practitioners. There are decisions that resemble exercises in problem-solving that necessitate extensive information gathering, with the ultimate aim of making a choice (Melucci, 1996:45).

No system can fully eliminate risk. Understanding risk involves judgment and balance. To manage risks, social workers and other professionals must make decisions with the best interests of the child in mind and within a timescale that has the child's safety as its paramount concern.

In any assessment of risk it is imperative that the child who is the subject of concern is seen. It almost feels an obvious statement, but the importance of placing the child at the centre of any assessment does need to be made explicit and this means the qualified social worker themselves must see the child. Again applying the welfare checklist (s. 1(3) CA89) is a good starting place for the social worker who must be satisfied, having seen the child, that they can competently address each component of the checklist. Importantly, the social worker must be able to ascertain the wishes and feelings of the child, assess the child's understanding of his or her own situation and circumstances and demonstrate a detailed knowledge and understanding of all significant relationships for the child. The social worker must interview parents and/or caregivers and determine the wider social and environmental factors that might impact on them and their child. It is important where there is more than one parent/caregiver that they are interviewed separately and, where appropriate, jointly. It is crucial that fathers/male caregivers are involved equally from the onset. Notwithstanding the research evidence from Brid Featherstone and Claire Fraser (2012) that highlights a clear gender imbalance in child protection practice, this important issue is highlighted in the key case analysis that follows (see page 38).

Crucial to effective child protection work is obtaining a full and detailed history of the family at the point of referral. It is imperative that information is recorded accurately with a clear analysis of the findings of the assessment, and to evaluate possibly with other relevant professionals what help should be provided. Importantly, the key message here is to provide an analysis of the situation and evaluate options of help – this

> **KEY CASE ANALYSIS**

Re N (Parenting Assessment) [2012]

This case involved a father who appealed a decision whereby a further parenting assessment was refused. The facts in the case were as follows. The local authority was assessing the maternal aunt and there was opposition to a further assessment of the father as this would result in delay. The father challenged this decision as the assessment would be completed within four weeks and stated that this was important as regardless of the placement outcome the father would have contact with the child. The appeal was allowed. Their lordships commented that social workers still focus primarily on women and mothers to obtain information relating to children.

There is an important message here that men and fathers must be involved and included at all stages of an assessment. Failure to involve and include men will almost certainly result in an incomplete assessment of needs and risks. Men must not be invisible, and social workers must ensure appointments are arranged to take into consideration the availability of both parents, rather than focusing on women, who are often more accessible.

is not only crucial for the family, but will assist in determining what resources agencies will need to deploy in response to the assessment.

It is important that enquiries about the concerns of a child are undertaken in a way that minimizes distress for the child and family. Where children are required to be interviewed by the police and children's social care following a decision to undertake a joint interview of the child as part of any criminal investigation, professionals should follow the guidance set out in *Achieving Best Evidence in Criminal Proceedings: Guidance for Vulnerable or Intimidated Witnesses, including Children* (Home Office, 2006).

Where there is a risk to the life of a child or a likelihood of serious immediate harm, local authority social workers, the police or the NSPCC should use their statutory child protection powers to act quickly to secure the immediate safety of the child. Importantly, where there are concerns regarding the safety of a child, the list of children who are subject to a child protection plan must be consulted. This is important to establish whether or not the child is already known to children's social care and the enquiry to the list will be recorded and will provide a vitally important source of information if, in the future, there are concerns which need to be investigated as it provides a chronology – where one incident by itself may not be sufficient, but a sequence of events may provide a very different picture.

Inevitably there will be referrals where concerns are not substantiated and the outcome of the enquiry needs to be conveyed by the social worker and their manager to the child, parents and other professionals. A decision needs to be made by the social worker as to whether the assessment is completed or if further assessment is required to determine the need for additional support services. Consideration may be given as to whether the child's health and development should be re-assessed regularly against specific objectives and who has responsibility for doing this.

There is an important role for other professionals who should be available to participate in further discussions as necessary, contribute to the completion of the assessment as appropriate, and provide services as identified in the plan for the child and family. The timescale for the assessment to reach a decision on next steps should be based on the needs of the individual child, consistent with the local protocol and no longer than 45 working days from the point of referral into local authority children's social care (DfE, 2013:34).

Where during the course of the assessment concerns are substantiated, but the child is not considered to be continuing, or likely, to suffer significant harm, the local authority should consider whether to proceed to a child protection conference where it is known that a child has already suffered significant harm.

The findings of the s. 47 enquiry should be discussed with other professionals and a decision made on all the available evidence as to whether a child protection conference is required, or whether a plan for ensuring the child's future safety and welfare can be developed and implemented without the need for a child protection conference or a child protection plan. Other professionals may and should request that the local authority convene a conference if they have serious concerns that a child might not adequately be safeguarded.

Where concerns are substantiated, and the child is judged to be continuing or likely to suffer significant harm, the local authority must convene an initial child protection conference to enable professionals involved with the child and family, and the child and his or her family where appropriate and possible to do so, to assess all relevant information and plan how to safeguard and promote the welfare of the child. The conference must be held within 15 working days of the last strategy discussion, but the timing of the conference must respond to the urgency of the situation and the needs of the child (DfE, 2013:35). It is crucial that key professionals who have knowledge of the family are invited to attend the conference, and do in fact attend and contribute to the analysis, decision-making and any recommendations. Parents should be invited to participate where possible and appropriate to do so, unless there are grounds for excluding them. If a parent is not able to attend, the reasons for the conference and any information to be shared at the conference, including reports, should be provided to them several days prior to the conference to allow sufficient time for parents to respond to the concerns either by written or oral submissions to the conference. It is not acceptable for a parent to be shown reports/evidence on the day of the conference and be expected to contribute to the conference in any meaningful way. If it is decided that a child should attend the conference, the child will need support in preparing to attend in person or to provide representations through a third party to the conference.

It is crucially important that reports to be submitted for the conference on the child and family provide an analysis of risk and the local authority's recommendation. All too frequently there is an over-focus on descriptive accounts that do not assist the conference in making a decision on risk. The decision of a child protection conference is whether or not to include the child on a list of children who are in need of a child protection plan. This decision will be based on whether or not the child is at continuing risk of harm. The chair of the conference will decide the primary category of harm (physical, sexual, emotional abuse or neglect). The conference may make further recommendations which should be embedded within the plan and the conference should agree membership of the core group of people who are responsible for reviewing the plan before the next review conference to be held no later than three months after the initial conference and thereafter every six months.

On-the-spot question	Important decision-making should not be left to an individual. What constitutes an effective process for decision-making?

Assessments

Achieving a good assessment in child protection work requires the translation of knowledge, skill, competence and confidence into analysis and reflection. It requires the practitioner to have extensive knowledge of the family in its own environment, and not to rely exclusively on either observations which take place in formal settings (i.e. meetings/court) or information from other professionals as this will inevitably lead to assessments being risk averse. It is not surprising that the unprecedented high number of care cases since 2009 has coincided with what can be termed the 'Ofsted effect' – targets and recording are linear procedures which will never reflect the emergent order of the intricacies of family life which are complex and overlapping. A disproportionate amount of social work time continues to be spent in writing lengthy descriptive narratives that sit more comfortably in the context of a creative writing degree rather than a social work assessment. The focus of an assessment in child protection must be to assess risk and this requires a deep level of analysis.

The inquiry report into the death of Jasmine Beckford highlighted a number of concerns regarding social work practice with families where child abuse was a feature, including a failure to take account of 'high-risk' families (Blom-Cooper et al., 1985). In response, guidance was published by the DoH, *Protecting Children: A Guide for Social Workers Undertaking a Comprehensive Assessment* (1988), more familiarly referred to as the 'Orange Book'.(Bring back the orange book! At a recent conference of over 300 social work delegates, this statement was met with unanimous applause.) Notwithstanding some of the criticisms of this assessment tool which could be considered prescriptive, it nevertheless provided the opportunity to obtain a comprehensive assessment of the family – it did talk about risk, unlike the replacement guidance *Framework for the Assessment of Children in Need and their Families* (DOH, 2000). There was scope to depart from the rather prescriptive list of 161 questions, but to retain an understanding of the complexities of both individuals and relationships, and the process of completing the assessment in itself required this to be an ongoing engagement with the individual/family as opposed to an over reliance on third-hand information, migrated into electronic data sheets which focus on descriptive targets rather than conveying any meaningful understanding of the complexity of relationships or families.

Social work practitioners, who are tasked to carve out effective relationships with some of the most vulnerable parents and carers, have seen more and more of their time for essential relationship-based work eroded. Moreover, they operate in an increasingly regulated and restricted climate, characterized by the standardization of both assessment and response (timescales, formats, off-the-shelf parenting classes and so forth), and this is coupled with the diverting of scant resources to criminal justice and a more punitive climate for welfare (Grover, 2008).

More recent instruction for assessments are to be found in the *Framework for the Assessment of Children in Need and their Families* (DOH, 2000) and *Working Together to Safeguard Children: A Guide to Interagency Working to Safeguard and Promote the Welfare of Children* (DoH, 2006). The assessment framework is referred to in *Working Together* (DfE, 2013), but there is a less prescriptive timescale for the completion of the previous initial and core assessments which have been replaced by guidance for the completion of assessments in 45 working days from the point of referral into children's social care.

Following the recommendation of the Munro Report, *Working Together* (DfE, 2013) has moved away from a prescriptive timescale for the completion of assessments, but importantly stresses the need for timely decision-making for the child. Whilst it is a positive move to depart from the rigidity of prescriptive timescales which have resulted in assessments being treated as a *one-off* task rather than a process of assessment and re-assessment of the child's needs, we cannot underestimate the importance of timely decision-making and planning or, consequently, the damage to the child when drift is allowed to occur. Whilst it is commendable and reassuring that social workers should base timescales upon professional judgment and expertise, there needs to be careful planning and review built into the system to ensure that good analytical assessments are undertaken in a timescale appropriate for the child.

The recommendations of the Munro Report as stated above propose a departure from a culture of regulation and an encouragement of direct work with the family. Whilst the rhetoric is encouraging, in practice there remains a tension with regard to contact with the family, which should remain proportionate to the need to respond to the reporting demands of the organization.

A good social work assessment requires deep analysis and critical reflection of the developmental needs of the child (being able to address all the questions in the s. 1(3) CA89 welfare checklist) and importantly the level of risk the child is or is likely to be exposed to. Furthermore, the strengths of each individual within the family and the family collectively need to be highlighted. An assessment needs to comply with the rules of natural justice – to be reasonable, proportionate, justifiable and achieved with full consultation and participation from the child and family. An assessment is not an event, rather a process that is reviewed regularly and updated in response to changes and developments. The assessment should be sufficiently detailed to inform the decision as to whether a child is in need or is suffering or likely to suffer significant harm as defined in s. 31 CA89.

A child in need is defined in s. 17 CA89 as a child who is unlikely to reach or maintain a satisfactory level of health or development, or their health and development will be significantly impaired, without the provision of services, or children who are disabled. In these cases, assessments by a social worker are carried out under s. 17 CA89. The aim of the assessment is to gather information about both a child's developmental needs and the parents' capacity to meet these needs within their immediate and extended family. The assessment must inform decisions as to the support the child needs.

In the event that the local authority believes the child is suffering or likely to suffer significant harm, the local authority has a duty under s. 47 CA89 to make enquiries to decide what action must be taken, working together with other professionals who have knowledge of the child and his or her family. The social worker in consultation with managers will need to make the decision as to whether the child is in need of immediate protection pending the outcome of the assessment. In the event the social worker considers the child to be at immediate risk, the local authority will need to consider whether to apply for either an EPO or police protection. The decision as to whether the local authority should apply for an EPO or request the assistance of the police will largely be determined by the circumstances in each case and the level of risk. Further discussion regarding use of emergency orders is to be found in Chapter 3.

Should the local authority make an application under s. 31 CA89, where the child is made the subject of a care order, the local authority will be required to assess the child's needs which will form the basis of the care plan. In reality this process should take place well before the local authority makes an application for a care order, as a detailed assessment must have been undertaken in order to arrive at a decision that applying for a care order must be in the child's best interests as opposed to the child remaining living at home or elsewhere with the agreement of his or her parents.

Furthermore, if a child is accommodated under s. 20 CA89, the local authority has a statutory responsibility to assess the needs of the child and, in consultation with the child and the family, agree a care plan which establishes the services required to meet the child's needs.

Regardless of whether the child is the subject of a care order or accommodated under s. 20 CA89, the care plan must be detailed and informed by an assessment and understanding of the child's needs. It must also outline all the arrangements in respect of the child and how these will be reviewed. Importantly, there must also be a contingency plan.

An assessment by a social worker is required before the child returns home under the Care Planning, Placement and Case Review (England) Regulations 2010. These regulations came into force on 1 April 2011 and make provision about care planning for looked after children (i.e. children who are looked after by a local authority, whether or not they are in the care of the local authority by virtue of a care order) and associated matters. The prescriptive nature of the regulations requiring details of the local authority's care plan for the child should provide evidence of whether the necessary changes and improvements have been made to ensure the child's safety when the child returns home.

PRACTICE FOCUS

Returning to the case study of Nancy and Jasper (see page 13), Nancy's health has deteriorated and she will require a short period in hospital for further tests and treatment. Nancy would prefer Jasper to remain at home and continue to be cared for by the care staff who have assisted her with the care of Jasper since he was born. The private care agency is stating that it cannot continue to do this without Nancy being present. Nancy is refusing to allow Jasper to be accommodated even for a short period by foster carers as she feels this would be too distressing for Jasper. What options are available to the local authority and what are the implications for both Jasper and Nancy?

On-the-spot questions

1 How will you make a decision as to what is in the best interests of Jasper?
2 If you make an application for a care order, what will be in your care plan?

Home visits

A good assessment must reflect the importance of place; both in terms of the physical space, which is home to the child and family, and to undertaking the assessment, at least in part, in the family home that can provide a rich understanding of the routines, interactions and relationships of family members which the family may not easily recognize or be able to convey adequately to the social worker.

> If you didn't have all the procedures and all the admin, you could devote your time to working with families, but the way things have gone, it's less and less that you spend time with families. Even in child protection you are doing assessments and writing reports and making recommendations with only a **nodding acquaintance** with the family very often. [emphasis in original]
>
> *Holt and Kelly, 2012b*

Given national concerns about the accessibility or 'reach' of child protection services, it is important to consider the extent to which the 'modernization' of children's services facilitates or inhibits families who are seeking help and who may be hard to access. Research findings from a study by Karen Broadhurst, Chris Grover and Janet Jamieson (2009) suggest that the recent reconfiguration of the front door to improve efficiency of initial response teams, including the setting up of centralized call centres and the introduction of timescales, may have resulted in unintentional consequences.

The national performance indicator NI14 requires that local authorities reduce 'avoidable contact', prompting local authorities to pursue ever more efficient filtering processes. Related research has found that centralized hubs, often staffed by unqualified workers, whilst improving 'through put', were much criticized by social work teams on account of their inability to effectively rationalize initial contacts. Critics have also suggested that the impersonal, standardized (mass production) response of the call centre may deter vulnerable families (Broadhurst, Wastell et al., 2010; Wastell et al., 2010). With the introduction of hot-desking, home-working and the increasing bureaucratization of social work, spatial separation between worker and service is further increased (Ferguson, 2011).

Contact with families has moved from the home to impersonal spaces reserved for contact and meetings. The environment for making assessments of families has changed significantly over the last 20 years – the once familiar home location has become a place social workers avoid visiting. The *comfort zone* has increasingly moved, as described above, to the office with the increased use of data processing and the need to meet prescriptive timescales, leaving families *hard to reach* and the *front door* of children's social care increasingly moving to office space with minimal facilities in which to meet visitors – a place where families are not welcome. The importance of *reaching* families in their own environment cannot be underestimated. It is arguably impossible to undertake a detailed assessment of the child and family without visiting the family home to see the physical space and to observe important relationships, interactions and routines, which will take a quite different form outside of the private space of the home.

On-the-spot question	Do you have legal authority to undertake a home visit if a parent who has parental responsibility for the child refuses this?

Local Safeguarding Children Boards

Safeguarding and promoting the welfare of children requires effective coordination in every local area. Section 13 of the CA04 requires each local authority to establish an LSCB for its area and specifies the organizations and individuals (other than the local authority) that should be represented on LSCBs (DfE, 2013:58). LSCBs coordinate the work to safeguard children locally and monitor and challenge the effectiveness of local arrangements. Ultimately, effective safeguarding of children can only be achieved by putting children at the centre of the system, and by every individual and agency playing their full part, working together to meet the needs of our most vulnerable children (DfE, 2013:8). The functions of an LSCB are set out in primary legislation contained in ss 14 and 14(a) of the CA04 and the Local Safeguarding Children Board Regulations 2006.

The core objectives of the LSCB are as follows:

> a. co-ordinate what is done by each person or body represented on the Board for the purposes of safeguarding and promoting the welfare of children in the area of the authority; and b. ensure the effectiveness of what is done by each such person or body for that purpose.
>
> *DfE, 2013:58*

Safeguarding and promoting the welfare of children is defined as: protecting children from maltreatment; preventing impairment of children's health or development; ensuring that children are growing up in circumstances consistent with the provision of safe and effective care; and taking action to enable all children to have the best outcomes (DfE, 2013:7).

Highlighted in the recent publication of *Working Together* is the need for a culture of continuous learning and improvement across the organizations that work together to safeguard and promote the welfare of children, identifying opportunities to draw on what works and to promote good practice (DfE, 2013:66).

Effective safeguarding systems are child-centred. Failings in safeguarding systems are too often the result of losing sight of the needs and views of the children within them, or placing the interests of adults ahead of the needs of children (DfE, 2013:9).

Strategic partnerships need to have strong leadership that can keep LSCBs focused on identifying priorities and keeping them on target (Horwath and Morrison, 2007). LSCB chairs have a key responsibility to lead the LSCB and provide a sense of direction. They also have a central role in ensuring that the LSCB has an independent voice and operates effectively (Local Safeguarding Children Board Regulations 2006 s. 3.50:83). The chair needs to be of sufficient standing and expertise to gain both respect and authority from LSCB members (s. 3.50:83).

Membership of the LSCB should be named individuals representing local agencies who have a responsibility for safeguarding children in their area. It is important that members have a key strategic role within their own organization for promoting the welfare of children. They should be in senior positions which will allow them to speak with authority on behalf of their organizations, commit their organizations on policy and practice issues and, ultimately, hold their organizations to account in relation to safeguarding matters (further details of membership of LSCBs is outlined in chapter 3 of DfE, 2013).

A study by Alan France et al. (2010), *The Evaluation of Arrangements for Effective Operation of the New Local Safeguarding Children Boards in England: Final Report*, concluded that LSCBs have brought about improvements in inter-agency child protection practice. In particular, they identify a greater sense of shared responsibility for child protection in most areas; child protection is no longer seen as the sole concern of children's social care. LSCBs also appear to offer effective leadership and provide clearer priorities and there was evidence of a 'shared understanding of child safeguarding' (France, 2010:7). Significantly, the study concludes that most frontline staff appeared clear about their responsibilities for raising concerns about children they felt were suffering harm.

The study also identified areas where LSCBs are not functioning as effectively. In most cases, local agencies have not embraced the wider safeguarding agenda and the LSCBs remain, for the most part, exclusively focused on child protection. At the time the study was carried out, children's trusts (since abolished) existed in each area, and the authors felt that in many areas there needed to be greater clarity as to the respective roles between these two structures.

In this context, it was felt that local authorities have struggled to establish accountability mechanisms, especially for chairs of LSCBs. Governance arrangements, the authors argue, generally remain weak. Despite this, many chairs have provided strong leadership.

The relationship between the LSCB and sub-committees

> Everyone wants to be on the Board for some reason, and the message I give to people is that it is a dull place, where you actually want to be is on one of the sub-committees, because that's where the real work goes on ... for instance somebody from the Fire Brigade wants to be on the Board and my reply is that the links are not so much with the Board but with the prevention sub-committee ... so I do try and keep it as tight as possible.
>
> *LSCB chair in France et al., 2010:39*

The LSCB delegates work on subcommittees of the LSCB. It is the work of the subcommittees that underpin the work of the LSCB. Subcommittees are chaired by members of the LSCB whose role it is to communicate recommendations/actions of the committee to the LSCB. There are a number of committees, but I want to make brief reference to the Child Death Overview Committee before devoting more time to the work of the Serious Case Review Committee where there is learning for professionals.

Child deaths

A subcommittee of the LSCB usually undertakes reviews of child deaths. It is this committee which is responsible for reviewing the information available on all child deaths, and is accountable to the chair of the LSCB.

Each death of a child is a tragedy for his or her family (including any siblings), and subsequent enquiries/investigations should keep an appropriate balance between forensic and medical requirements and the family's need for support. A minority of unexpected deaths are the consequence of abuse or neglect or are found to have abuse or neglect as an associated factor. In all cases, enquiries should seek to understand the reasons for the child's death, address the possible needs of other children in the household, the needs of all family members, and also consider any lessons to be learnt about how best to safeguard and promote children's welfare in the future (DCSF, 2010, para. 7.4). There should be an SCR in certain cases where a child dies and the independent chair of the LSCB usually takes the decision as to whether the death of a child should prompt an SCR.

Serious case reviews

Regulation 5 of the Local Safeguarding Children Board Regulations 2006 requires LSCBs to undertake reviews of serious cases in the following circumstances. Firstly, where a child sustains a potentially life-threatening injury or serious and permanent impairment of health and development through abuse or neglect. Secondly, where a child has been seriously harmed as a result of being subject to sexual abuse. Thirdly, where a parent has been murdered and a domestic homicide review is being initiated. Fourthly, where a child has been seriously harmed following a violent assault perpetrated by another child or an adult, and the case gives rise to concerns about the way in which local professionals and services worked together to safeguard and promote the welfare of children. This includes inter-agency and/or interdisciplinary working.

The purpose of an SCR is for agencies and individuals to learn lessons to improve the way in which they work both individually and collectively to safeguard and promote the welfare of children (DfE, 2013:68). The lessons learned should be disseminated effectively, and the recommendations should be implemented in a timely manner so that the changes required result, wherever possible, in children being protected from suffering or being likely to suffer harm in the future. It is essential, to maximize the quality of learning, that the child's daily life experiences and an understanding of his or her welfare, wishes and feelings are at the centre of the SCR, irrespective of whether the child died or was seriously harmed. This perspective should inform the scope and terms of reference of the SCR as well as the ways in which the information is presented and addressed at all stages of the process, including the conclusions and recommendations.

Reviews vary in their breadth and complexity but, in all cases, where possible lessons should be acted upon quickly without necessarily waiting for the SCR to be completed. Any professional or agency may refer a case to the LSCB if they believe that there are important lessons for intra- and/or inter-agency working to be learned from the case.

An SCR is not an inquiry into how a child died or was seriously harmed or into who is culpable, as these are matters for the coroners' courts and criminal courts.

Learning lessons from serious case reviews

Ten common pitfalls

As a member of an LSCB, SCR committee and former Area Child Protection Committee and Part 8 Review Committee for over 25 years, the author has identified a number of recurrent themes that emerge from SCRs where lessons can be learned. These are important messages that should inform your practice. They are referred to here as the ten most common *pitfalls* that feature in every single SCR spanning three decades of involvement in this work. Despite all the research in this area and the resources deployed in SCRs (Parton, 2004), sadly the findings and learning identified in the most recent SCR is almost identical to the first SCR attended by the author in 1987. (Pitfalls is a concept used by Broadhurst and White et al., 2010.)

1 History and understanding of parenting behaviours is pivotal to a good assessment but it is often absent when examining SCR documentation. It is important to know about the parents' or other caregivers' history – including their own experience of being parented, past and potential patterns of behaviour or concerns – to identify

factors which may point to enhanced risk or which may be protective. In addition, it is important to assess the impact on the parent of behaviours in the wider family network. This did not necessarily rule out capacity to change but, where families were overwhelmed and struggling in an adverse environment, professionals need support to identify parental behaviour harmful to a child. Past history is a good indicator of future behaviour and it is crucial that social workers obtain a full and detailed history of parenting behaviour and make an analysis of the information in terms of risk to the child (Broadhurst, Wastell et al., 2009).

2 Fixed thinking prevents understanding of a child's changing circumstances. It is interesting to read documents where professionals have met regularly over a significant period of time at conferences and core group meetings. During this period, notwithstanding multiple setbacks and new information/evidence which significantly increases the risk to the child, professionals hold on to the original plan: *'One of the most common, problematic tendencies in human cognition ... is our failure to review judgments and plans – once we have formed a view on what is going on, we often fail to notice or to dismiss evidence that challenges that picture.'* (Fish et al., 2008:9) There is clear evidence of the *start-again syndrome* with parents given a fresh opportunity to *start again* with the plan even where the plan is clearly not working and not in the child's best interests. The original decision is supported and reinforced by the group of professionals who originally agreed the plan. Commentators (notably Kelly, 2002) refer to this as *group think.* Group think is both powerful and pervasive and must be recognized by professionals who are working together with complex families. Fixed thinking and group think often reflect an over-focusing on descriptive material and a lack of analysis of the situation as a whole (Kelly, 2002; Sinclair and Bullock, 2002; Sidebotham, 2012).

3 The child remains invisible. Whilst this must be difficult to comprehend following the messages contained in the reports of Lord Laming and Professor Munro, despite this there are still too many instances of the child remaining invisible. As part of a pilot study in 2008–2010, Holt attended over 30 pre-proceedings meetings where there were serious concerns about the protection of children. In every meeting the parents were present, but not the child; there was representation for the parent, but no representation for the child; and there was a

consistent over-focus on the presenting issues/needs of the adult whilst the child remained largely invisible. It is understandable and entirely appropriate that social workers consider each parent and their capacity to parent, but this must never be at the expense of not addressing the needs of the child and being in a position to put forward the child's needs/wishes as outlined in the welfare checklist discussed in Chapter 1 (Reder et al., 1993; Cooper, 2005).

4 Children are insufficiently consulted or spoken with – siblings of the index child and young people living outside of the home are not interviewed or assessed. Social workers fall short when assessing children with complex needs/disabilities, often focusing on the disability and the parent's capacity to cope rather than assessing what is *good enough* for this particular child who may require a higher standard of care, but nevertheless the higher standard of care may be just *good enough*. No apologies are made for stating that our child protection procedures and practices must protect the most vulnerable of our children for them to be effective. If our procedures and practices do not protect children with the most complex needs, they are not working (Ofsted, 2012). In respect of older children, practitioners often consider them to be *hard to help*. Young people are also vulnerable and may be *hard to reach*, but we must reach them and find ways of engaging them in assessments (Lefevre, 2010).

5 There is lack of information about fathers or male figures in assessments. Fathers are most visible in the child protection system when they are implicated in the suspected abuse. Philip Gilligan et al. (2011), Featherstone et al. (2010) and Featherstone (2009) suggest a need for change in the approach to fathers in the child protection system. Perceptions of men as *troublesome* in the context of child protection are a prevailing feature; their absence, for example, is usually interpreted negatively rather than examined in the context of how professionals may positively target women and ignore men. Assessments must always involve and include men and consider how fathers can play an important role in the lives of children. In respect of men who are regarded as *troublesome*, there is a need to examine how organizations respond to men who present a risk but who may be hard to reach (Reissman and Quinney, 2005).

The important message here is that men must not remain invisible – social workers must work with men and involve them fully in all assessments.

6 Agency *capacity and climate* must be considered within assessments and in discussions within organizations. How information is used is often critical – there needs to be an openness about the organizational culture that places more emphasis on gathering information rather than understanding it. Whilst the rhetoric of the policymakers is laudable in terms of promoting the need to be more reflective and analytical, this needs to be translated and prioritized within organizations. We need to move away from a *cut-and-paste culture* to thinking critically and analytically and this takes time, experience, confidence and training (Broadhurst and Holt, 2010).

The chaotic behaviour in families was often mirrored in professionals' thinking and actions. Many families and professionals were overwhelmed by having too many problems to face and too much to achieve. These circumstances contributed to the child being lost or unseen. The capacity to understand the ways in which children are at risk of harm is complex and requires clear thinking.

7 Multiple risks require a transactional/ecological perspective: 'An ecological-transactional perspective views child development as a progressive sequence of age- and stage-appropriate tasks in which successful resolution of tasks at each developmental level must be co-ordinated and integrated with the environment, as well as with subsequently emerging issues across the lifespan. These tasks include the development of emotion regulation, the formation of attachment relationships, the development of an autonomous self, symbolic development, moral development, the formation of peer relationships, adaptation to school, and personality organization ... Poor resolution of stage-salient issues may contribute to maladjustment over time as prior history influences selection, engagement, and interpretation of subsequent experience ...' (Cicchetti and Valentino, 2006:143)

In most SCRs there are co-existing factors, notably mental health, substance misuse and domestic abuse. It is important that social workers are able to analyse interacting risk factors using an ecological and transactional perspective. It is important to understand parental psychology, historical context and to provide a dynamic and analytical assessment that is not incident-driven (Gibbons et al.; 1995; Hindley et al., 2006).

8 Rule of optimism: whilst social workers do need to highlight the positive aspects of individuals and the family, as well as identifying areas

for improvement, adopting the rule of optimism is something quite different. The rule of optimism is in many ways similar to fixed thinking that is discussed above. It is the inability to step back and reflect on the information/evidence available and to be clear about risk. This may also result from overwhelmed workers who have so many problems to face in terms of the nature of the work and too much to achieve in terms of the demands of both overwhelmed families and overstretched organizations (Bunting and Reid, 2005). Practitioners who are overwhelmed, not just by the volume of work but also by its nature, may not be able to do even the simple things well. Good support, supervision and a fully staffed workforce are crucial.

9 Parental cooperation is often not effectively or robustly scrutinized. There is evidence of much parental resistance that is left unchallenged. Resistance can manifest itself in many ways but some families avoid professionals with multiple moves that result in many children going off the radar of social workers. Barlow and Scott (2010:57) state: '*Lack of cooperation on the part of families is a key factor preventing effective assessment and needs to be included as a key indication of risk in the assessment process. Lack of cooperation should be used to justify compulsory interventions.*'

In order to overcome the resistance and lack of candour, practitioners need to have the skills to develop and maintain relationships and have a well-developed capacity for empathy with adults whilst retaining a focus on risks to children. It is also well recognized that in order for practitioners to work in this way they need highly skilled supervision to provide additional insights on the family, space and opportunity for reflection in and on practice and emotional support to workers who are intervening with emotionally demanding families.

Alternatively, perceived *good parental engagement* or *compliance* with organizational goals sometimes masks risks of harm to the child (Reder and Duncan, 1999; Bostock et al., 2005).

10 Poor communication within and between agencies features at some level in every case. In some agencies, there is poor communication between colleagues working for the same organization and working in close physical proximity – this problem has increased with the use of digital technology that often replaces conversations and office talk. The culture of the office has changed with qualified social workers relying heavily on text and email communication rather than talking. Management supervision is largely about checking that the

correct data has been recorded and timescales met, which has become commonplace in formatted data surveillance documents, rather than focusing on a deep analysis of the descriptive material (Wastell et al., 2010). It is essential that practitioners are underpinned by skilled supervision that supports them in the challenging task of working with complex families. When working with complex and challenging families, especially when resources are limited and professionals feel pressured, it is essential that practitioners have access to skilled supervision to support challenge, reflection and professional development, but also to provide emotional support and opportunities for personal development. It is particularly important when practitioners feel overwhelmed and lack confidence, especially when this leads to a failure to take key decisions. Supervisors need to help practitioners have a sense of direction to keep them on track, especially giving thought to whether the current approach is working and to maintain a clear record of decision-making.

Practitioners require the skills to develop collaborative working relationships with colleagues from other agencies when perspectives and priorities differ and a challenge of the professional perspective or activity is required. There are times when professional, inter-agency challenges need to be supported by clear procedures to address them. Successful interagency collaborative working is underpinned by structures such as child protection conferences and other inter-agency forums. It is essential that practitioners are given the opportunities and tools necessary to contribute effectively. Procedures and guidance with respect to arrangements, including timescales, for convening of child protection conferences and other inter-agency meetings must be followed if they are to be effective in safeguarding children. In order to foster good inter-agency working relationships there are times when it is essential that there is a multi-agency forum in which practitioners can explore their perspectives and challenges in their work with families.

Assessments and working with others

Government guidance stresses that the task of safeguarding children and promoting their welfare is a joint responsibility to be shared by a range of agencies, all with different areas of expertise (DfE, 2013). However, past research identifies a number of obstacles to inter-agency working, including fragmentation of service responsibilities, differences in values, variable understanding of other professionals' roles and tensions concerning status, autonomy and professional expertise (Hardy et al., 1992; Easen et al., 2000; Hudson, 2000; Hudson et al., 2003; Murphy, 2004). Role confusion was also identified as undermining effective inter-agency collaboration (Calder and Barratt, 1997). The implementation of LSCBs was one of a range of measures intended to address some of these difficulties.

A consistent message from research, which has been reinforced in every high-profile inquiry on child protection, is that children are best protected when professionals are clear about what is required of them individually and how they need to work together.

> For inter-agency working to be effective professionals need to find ways of overcoming professional boundaries and tensions caused by differences in professional cultures. Involving and engaging a wide range of agencies in safeguarding children is recognised to be challenging but has the potential to support the development of new practices and enhance the decision-making process
>
> *France et al., 2010:99*

It is important that children receive the right help at the right time. For that to happen, everyone who comes into contact with them has to play a role in identifying concerns early, sharing information and taking prompt, informed action. This will involve a range of professionals – for example, midwives, health visitors, general practitioners, early years professionals, teachers, police officers, youth workers, voluntary workers and social workers. It will require all professionals to be vigilant and take prompt action when they suspect that a child is suffering harm (DfE, 2013).

Section 10 CA04 requires each local authority to make arrangements to promote cooperation between the authority, each of the authority's relevant partners and such other persons or bodies working with children in the local authority's area as the authority considers appropriate. The arrangements are to be made with a view to improving the well-being of all children in the authority's area – which includes protection from harm or neglect alongside other outcomes.

One of the reasons why the system has let down children in the past is because key people and bodies coming into contact with children on a regular basis often fail to give sufficient priority to safeguarding and promoting the welfare of children. Section 11 CA04, s. 175 Education Act 2002, s. 40 Childcare Act 2006 and s. 55 Borders, Citizenship and Immigration Act 2009 place duties on organizations and individuals to ensure that their functions are discharged with regard to the need to safeguard and promote the welfare of children.

Summary

There are tensions and dilemmas in relation to where the boundaries of decision-making lie in relation to the most complex cases. Although the government response to the *Family Justice Review* (MoJ, 2011) places parents and children at the heart of the process, on close examination of the proposals the emphasis appears to be on cutting costs and standard-izing court timescales. The aspirations of the policy-makers to reduce delay for children is consistent with the principles of the CA89, and clearly in the best interests of children, but the rhetoric does not appear to be supported with any additional resources for local authorities who are already saddled with resource constraints and, despite the Munro recommendations, appear to have no less regulation and bureaucracy to navigate.

The rights of children and parents to participate and be represented in decision-making in child protection practice have always presented difficulty. It is accepted that the aspirations of the policy and legislative mandates to achieving consensual solutions in safeguarding children are laudable, as is the wish to keep the rights of children and parents at the heart of the process, but we can see that the messages from research into SCRs highlight how often the rhetoric is not supported in practice.

Participation, knowledge and representation for parents in child protection processes is pivotal – decisions are being made about whether children should remain living with their parents or be removed from their parents' care on a compulsory basis. These decisions are life-changing for children and their families, and by definition often come at a stage where the local authority feels it cannot continue to work in partnership or by agreement. The *Family Justice Review* (MoJ, 2011) highlights the need for the most experienced of social work professionals to be involved in complex child protection cases, but ever-increasing volumes of work and no relief from the administrative burden makes the task of engaging with hard to reach families challenging.

Whilst the rhetoric of legal and policy mandates to provide consensual solutions wherever possible and safe to do so within the context of child protection may be well intentioned, the challenge remains in relation to all professionals involved in the process to ensure children and parents are properly represented when important decisions are being made. This is particularly important in a context of extensive public sector cuts and a move to proportionate working practices amongst key professionals.

Further reading

Brandon, M, S Bailey, P Belderson, R Gardner, P Sidebottom, J Dodsworth, C Warren and J Black (2009) *Understanding Serious Case Reviews and their Impact: A Biennial Analysis of Serious Case Reviews 2005–2007*. This book provides in-depth analysis from a biennial review of SCRs to facilitate learning and to promote good practice in safeguarding children and working together.

Davy, C (2010) *Children's Participation in Decision-making: A Summary Report on Progress Made up to 2010*. This focuses on the importance of involving children in the decision-making process.

Department for Education (2013) *Working Together to Safeguard Children*. A revised and concise important guidance document that should be read by practitioners from all agencies who work together to safeguard children.

Ferguson, H (2011) *Child Protection Practice*. This provides a detailed account of the challenges of current child protection practice.

Munro, E (2011) *The Munro Review of Child Protection Final Report: A Child-centred System*. Arguably one of the most important reports, this provides a comprehensive review of child protection practice with a clear message that children should remain at the heart of the system for which Munro must be commended.

3

EMERGENCY APPLICATIONS/ SHORT-TERM MEASURES

AT A GLANCE THIS CHAPTER COVERS:

- political climate
- emergency applications
- alternative ways of handling an emergency

Political climate

Achieving consensual solutions in order to prevent children from coming into care is desirable when appropriate and safe to do so. However, there are times when the local authority must seek an order to remove a child who '*is suffering or is likely to suffer significant harm*' (s. 31(2)(1) CA89). There has been a sharp rise in the number of care proceedings reported since 2009. This sharp increase has been largely attributed to the 'Baby Peter Effect' (Gillen, 2009) and there is no doubt that the death of baby Peter Connelly, in the context of a child welfare culture characterized by 'error and blame' (White and Broadhurst, 2009), will have served to resolve many cases of children on the edge of care.

> Helping children, families and adults who are in crisis or in difficult or dangerous situations to be safe, to cope and take control of their lives again requires exceptional professional judgment. Social workers have to be highly skilled in their interactions and must draw on a sound professional understanding of social work. They have to be able to do all of this while sustaining strong partnerships with the children or adults they are working with and their families: sometimes they will be the only people offering the stability and consistency that is badly needed.
>
> Munro Report, *Munro, 2011:30*

Whilst the rhetoric of achieving strong partnerships with families is laudable, these aspirations are difficult for social workers to achieve in the context of a profession that continues to see an increase in regulation and bureaucracy (Broadhurst and Holt, 2010). Working with children and their families who are in crisis is arguably one of the most complex areas of work. Assessing risk and making informed decisions is crucial in this area of work, and it requires skill, expertise, experience and good judgment, supported by a whole-system approach.

An effective family justice system is therefore needed to support the making of these important decisions. It must be one that provides both children and families with an opportunity to have their own views heard in the decisions that will be made; provides proper safeguards to ensure vulnerable children and families are protected; enables and encourages out-of-court resolution, where this is appropriate; and ensures there is proportionate and skilfully managed court involvement (Masson, 2011a). Public law childcare decisions are life changing for children and their families and there is a need for the most experienced of social work and legal professionals to be involved in this process (*Family Justice Review*, MoJ, 2011a).

Emergency applications

If it is urgent and of necessity to either keep in or remove a child to a place of safety, a local authority should wherever possible, and unless a child's safety is otherwise at immediate risk, apply for an EPO. *Working Together* says police powers to remove a child in an emergency should be used only in exceptional circumstances where there is insufficient time to seek an EPO or for reasons relating to the immediate safety of the child (DoH, 2000: para. 5.51).

Police protection

There will be situations where the assistance of the police will be required in an emergency to remove a child to a place of safety. This must be a real emergency, and the action is necessary to secure the immediate safety of the child where there is actual or imminent danger to the child and to delay removing the child by seeking an EPO could lead to serious injury or death.

The police have to agree and they need to be satisfied that the grounds below for taking this action are met. Where a constable has reasonable cause to believe that a child would otherwise be likely to suffer significant harm, he or she may:

46(1)

    (a) remove the child to suitable accommodation and keep him there; or
    (b) take such steps as are reasonable to ensure that the child's removal from any hospital, or other place, in which he is then being accommodated is prevented.

CA89

There is clear guidance provided to the police on how to exercise their powers (Home Office, 1989). Police protection lasts for a maximum period of 72 hours (s. 46(6) CA89), but must be terminated as soon as the danger to the child has passed (s. 46(5) CA89). The police must take reasonable steps to inform the child, his or her parents, anyone else who has parental responsibility and the person the child was living with at the time of the removal of the action taken, the reason for it and the next stage (s. 46(4) CA89). The police officers' duties are to inform the local authority where the child is found and of where he ordinarily resides if the two are different (s. 46(3)(a)–(b) CA89) *'and take such steps as are reasonably practicable to discover the wishes and feelings of the child'* (s. 46(3)(d) CA89).

Police protection immediately triggers the duty to investigate (s. 47 CA89), which will involve the local authority considering whether to continue with the order and to make an assessment of where the child should reside whilst any further assessments are being undertaken. It is worthy to note here that the police have powers under the common law to arrest a person and remove them from the property if there is a risk to life and limb or a breach of the peace (Police and Criminal Evidence Act 1984).

Emergency protection orders

When considering whether emergency action is necessary, legal advice should be obtained and a strategy discussion held to consider the needs of the specific child, but also the needs of other children in the same household or in the household of an alleged perpetrator. Given the emergency nature of this application, consideration will need to be given urgently as to the availability of suitable accommodation for each child.

The responsibility for taking emergency action rests with the local authority in whose area the child is found, where the circumstances require emergency action. If the local authority establishes the child is looked after by, or is the subject of, a child protection plan in another authority, it is the local authority where the child is found that should consult the authority responsible for the child. Only when the original local authority explicitly accepts responsibility in writing is the local authority where the child is found relieved of its responsibility to take emergency action.

44

(1) Where any person applies to the court for an order to be made, the order may be made if;
   (a) there is reasonable cause to believe that the child is likely to suffer significant harm if:

(i)   he is not removed to accommodation provided by or on behalf of the applicant; or

(ii) he does not remain in the place in which he is then being accommodated.

CA89

The order lasts for eight days (s. 45(1) CA89) and in exceptional circumstances may be renewed for a further seven days (s. 45(5) CA89).

Whilst an order is in force it:

44(4)(b)

(i)   authorizes the removal of the child at any time to accommodation provided by or on behalf of applicant and his being kept there; or

(ii) the prevention of the child's removal from any hospital, or other place, in which he was being accommodated immediately before the making of the order; and gives the applicant parental responsibility for the child.

CA89

One of the grounds for an EPO lies in the duty to investigate under s. 47 CA89. If during an investigation access to the child is unreasonably refused, the local authority may apply for an EPO (s. 44 (1)(b) CA89). Planned emergency action will normally take place following a strategy discussion or meeting, involving as a minimum the social worker, manager and the police. Social workers, the police or NSPCC should initiate a strategy discussion as soon as possible to discuss planned emergency action (*Working Together,* DfE, 2013:23).

It is imperative that the child is seen (this should be undertaken by a practitioner from the agency initiating the emergency action) to decide how best to protect the child and whether an application for an EPO is the most appropriate means of achieving this. Wherever possible it is good practice to obtain legal advice at the earliest opportunity to discuss the evidence and to alert the court of the intention to make an application for an EPO. This is good practice as it will allow an opportunity for the applicant to discuss the evidence for the application and to ensure that the court has sufficient notice of the application and appropriate court personnel are available to deal with the application.

In exceptional circumstances an EPO may be made *ex parte* – the court will allow the application to be made without all parties being in court. The decision to make an *ex parte* application must take account of the rights of the parent(s) as well as the child, although it is the welfare of the child that must remain paramount. The only justifiable reasons for not informing a parent/person with parental responsibility of an intention to make an application for an EPO is if to do so would put the child at further and imminent risk. There are important rules for applications without notice to be found in Proceedings Relating to Children Except Parental Order Proceedings and Proceedings for Applications in Adoptions Placement and Related Proceedings (Family Procedure Rules (FPR) Part 12). Where an EPO is made without notice, the applicant must serve a copy of the application on each parent/person with parental responsibility within 48 hours of the emergency order being made, unless the court directs otherwise. Should the court refuse to make an order on an application without notice it may direct that the application is made on notice in which case the application will proceed in accordance with r. 12.3 to r. 12.15.

A parent or person with parental responsibility may apply for a discharge of the EPO after 72 hours, providing that they were not present at the original hearing (r. 12.3). There is also the power to include an exclusion requirement in the EPO (s. 44A(1) CA89) where there is reasonable cause to believe that, if a person is excluded from a dwelling house in which the child lives, the child will not be likely to suffer significant harm (s. 44A(2) CA89).

It is good practice where it is appropriate and safe to do so to advise parents or those with parental responsibility to seek immediate legal advice when a decision has been made to apply for an EPO and always when an EPO is served. Importantly, the child must be seen and his or her wishes and feelings must be ascertained as soon as possible in an emergency situation.

In a situation where a child is subject to an EPO, and children's social care wishes to remove the child and that removal is obstructed, the local authority can consider an application for a recovery order (s. 50 CA89).

The child's parents, anyone with parental responsibility, or anyone with whom the child was living prior to the EPO being made should be notified that an application is to be made for an EPO unless it is not in the child's best interests to do so. Legal advice must be obtained before embarking on this course of action, as the evidence must be challenged at the earliest opportunity, to ensure the rights of the child and relevant adults are protected and the action being proposed is both proportionate and reasonable.

The social worker applying for the order must have clear plans regarding the duration of the order, where the child should reside and any contact arrangements and with whom before an application is made. The emergency nature of this application is such that the social worker will need to have given consideration to all these issues as within hours the child and his parents/carers will be seeking clarification on what will happen next. The situation will be highly charged and often acrimonious and not having a clear plan will only contribute to further distress for the child and his or her family. In accordance with the guidance in *Working Together* (DfE, 2013:18), it is important that all assessments, decisions and plans are clearly recorded in a timely manner. Furthermore, the LSCB should publish a threshold document (DfE, 2013:14) that includes the process for the early help assessment and the type and level of early help services to be provided which may be helpful to agencies which have concerns regarding a child's welfare.

The unplanned removal of children from the care of their parents continues to evoke intense political, judicial and public debate. The media has contributed to this immensely contentious area of child care practice with images of young babies being removed from their parents and the release of figures from Cafcass showing that, between April and August 2012, Cafcass received a total of 4489 applications. This figure is 8.5 per cent higher when compared to the same period in the previous year and with no sign of this pattern abating. Despite the concern regarding the number of children who are removed from their parents, there is equal outrage by high-profile cases such as the tragic death of Peter Connelly, where there has been criticism when it appears that children were not removed who should have been.

Firstly, and importantly, in the absence of police protection (s. 46 CA89) or a court order authorizing removal or informed consent of a parent (s. 20 CA89), the local authority is not entitled to remove a child from the care of a parent. This was clearly stated in *R v Nottingham City Council* [2008].

The removal of a child from his or her parents is a very serious step and the consequences for the child are considerable. The court should always consider the least restrictive option before ordering the removal of a child unless there are cogent reasons to do so, as in the case of *Re O (A Child: Supervision Order: Future Harm)* [2001]. The premature removal of a baby on the basis of future risk was severely criticized in *Re C and B (Care Order: Future Harm)* [2001]. The court acknowledged that in some cases removal on the basis on future harm was acceptable, but this must be based on the nature and gravity of harm and the court found there to be insufficient evidence in this case to warrant such action.

In *Re G (Care: Challenge to Local Authority's Decision)* [2003], Munby J held: 'The fact that a local authority has parental responsibility for children pursuant to s 33(3)(a) of the Children Act 1989 does not entitle it to take decisions about children without reference to, or over the heads of the children's parents.' In this case Munby stated that the local authority should not be entitled to remove a child without firstly properly consulting and involving the parent in the decision-making process. Whilst it was acknowledged that the local authority had parental responsibility for the child, the parent also shared parental responsibility and this should be acknowledged and respected.

The making of an order to remove a child from his or her family should take into consideration the ECHR and a court must only make such an order if it is both *necessary* and *proportionate* and there was no other alternative to promoting the welfare of the child as was stated in *Re B (Care: Interference with Family Life)* [2003].

There is considerable authority to support the indisputable proposition that Article 8 ECHR has both a *substantive* and a *procedural* component. The substantive component regulates the circumstances in which a public authority can interfere with private or family life; the procedural component imposes upon the public authority the obligation of proper consultation with the family before it interferes. It is upon this latter obligation that we initially focus.

The first point – and this is crucial – is that Article 8 applies not merely to *judicial* but also to *administrative* decision-making. Focusing on child protection, Article 8 guarantees fairness in the decision-making process, and that the procedural safeguards afforded by Article 8 apply, at *all* stages of the process, both in and out of court. So parents have a right to be fully involved in the planning by public authorities of public authority intervention in the lives of their family and their children, *before* care proceedings have been commenced, *during* the proceedings, as well as *after* the final care order has been made (Mumby, 2009). The emphasis is clearly on *before* as well as during and after the care proceedings. Hence, the duty of the local authority to engage with parents, fully and frankly, in the pre-proceedings and, if the child is not yet born, in the pre-birth planning and decision-making process – to be found in the decision in *Bury MBC v D* [2009]:

> It is elementary that under Article 8 of the Convention parents have a right to be fully involved in the planning by public authorities of public authority intervention in the lives of their family and their children, whether before, during or after care proceedings, the emphasis for present circumstances obviously being upon that element of the obligation under Article 8 which arises before the commencement of the proceedings.
>
> Bury MBC v D *[2009] para. 7*

Bury MBC v D was a case involving pre-birth planning for the removal of a child at birth, so the process did not involve s. 47 CA89. However, the same principles should apply equally to s. 47 investigations. However, the ECtHR gives a 'wide margin of appreciation' to decisions made by child protection authorities to separate parents and children temporarily as evidenced in *L v Finland* [2000]. The court has accepted that the child's welfare can justify action that might otherwise breach the parents' rights. In *Johansen v Norway* (1996) it was stated that a 'fair balance' has to be struck between the interests of parent and child, and a parent is not entitled to have action taken which would jeopardize the welfare of the child.

Human rights challenges to state intervention in child protection cases are frequently decided on the basis of Article 8, rather than Article 6(1). Article 8 requires that parents are 18 years of age. Parents need to be sufficiently involved in decisions about their children before, during and after any proceedings, which may curtail the exercise of their rights as parents. Where the court has found that parents' Article 8 rights have been infringed, it has often not considered Article 6, stating that it raises no further points as was the case in *Venema v The Netherlands* [2003].

On this basis, it is accepted that child protection authorities may legitimately remove a child who is believed to be at serious risk of harm from his or her parents. The court has also accepted that the power to do this may be obtained administratively, either abruptly as in *K and T v Finland* [2000], or with limited evidence as in *P, C and S v UK* [2002]

In the course of setting out a number of guiding principles in relation to EPOs, in *Re X Council v B (Emergency Protection Orders)* [2005] Munby J held that: 'Separation is only to be contemplated if immediate separation is essential to secure the child's safety: "imminent danger" must be "actually established".' (Appendix B) Furthermore, he added that an application for an EPO should be approached with an anxious awareness of the extreme gravity of the impact of the making of such an order on the rights of both the child and family. The importance of independent representation to challenge this decision was highlighted in the late appointment of the **family court advisor** (FCA). It was regarded as unacceptable in an application for an EPO that the appointment of the FCA was delayed by 10 days. An EPO was a 'draconian' and 'extremely harsh' measure, requiring 'exceptional justification' and 'extraordinarily compelling reasons' (Appendix B). It should not be made unless the Family Proceedings Court is satisfied that it is both necessary and proportionate and that no other less radical form of order would promote the welfare of the child.

Moreover, consideration needs to be given as to whether the making of an EPO is proportionate to the remedy being sought and the evidence of the local authority should be detailed and compelling with parents given notice of the proceedings and intention of the local authority, except in exceptional circumstances. The local authority should always consider whether an application for a child assessment order (s. 43 CA89) is a more appropriate application if the intention of the local authority is to undertake an assessment. An *ex parte* application should only be sought if there is a genuine emergency, but in most cases, unless the child's welfare would be compromised, parents should be given notice of the application and proceedings. Following the making of an EPO, the local authority remains under an obligation to consider less drastic alternatives to emergency removal. Section 44 imposes a duty on the local authority to keep the case under review daily to ensure the parent and child are separated for no longer than is necessary to secure the child's safety. Arrangements for 'reasonable contact' during the time the order is in force, required under s. 44 (13), have to be needs-led and not resource-driven.

The case was followed in *Re X: Emergency Protection Orders* [2006] with further directions for emergency orders. McFarlane J added that all Family Proceedings Courts should have a copy of the judgment of Munby J in *Re X* and refer to it in all applications for an EPO. Furthermore, and significantly for practice, the absence of knowledge should never be the basis for the making of an EPO, nor should cases of either emotional abuse, sexual abuse, or fabricated illness without specific evidence of immediate and direct risk of physical harm to the child.

> → **KEY CASE ANALYSIS** ←

Re L (A Child) [2007]

In *Re L (A Child)* [2007] the local authority, supported by the FCA, sought to remove a child prior to the final order being made. There was an undisputed risk of harm from the mother's partner, and in response the mother was seeking a residential assessment. The judge supported the mother's application and was critical of the local authority application for making an assumption that, as long as the interim threshold was met, the court should support removal of the child. The judgment in this case provides some clear principles for practitioners as detailed below.

1 The court must consider whether there is an imminent risk of really serious harm that warrants immediate removal of the child (per Thorpe LJ in *Re H (A Child) (Interim Care Order)* [2003].
2 If there is no imminent risk of really serious harm, the question of a parent's ability to provide good enough long-term care is a matter for the court at the final hearing and should not be sought at an interim stage, as this effectively prejudices a fair trial.
3 Professionals conflate the test to be applied to the issue of removal and the nature and extent of the risk of harm (which will only justify removal if there is an imminent risk of really serious harm, not just a heightened perception of risk as evidence emerges if that risk can be contained by adequate arrangements).

Applying the principles from the cases cited above, a local authority and a court should consider:

1 Whether there is reasonable justification for an order interfering with the child's right to family life.
2 If there are any concerns, the court and local authority should take the least restrictive approach with alternatives explored before the option of removal taken. The local authority needs to consider whether there is clear established evidence of immediate risk of really serious harm or imminent danger, which cannot be reduced without removal of the child.
3 The court needs to be satisfied that the parents have been properly involved in the decision-making of the local authority or afforded the proper opportunity to make their case before a decision is made.

4 There may be extraordinarily compelling reasons which exceptionally might justify the removal of a child under an EPO.

5 An order for the assessment of a child is not in itself sufficient justification for removal.

6 Evidence in support of the removal of a child must be full, detailed, precise and compelling.

7 There need to be clear and detailed proposals for contact arrangements between the child and his or her parents.

8 The court will need all relevant documents, including child protection conference minutes, and will need to be satisfied that the parents have seen all relevant documents.

9 The court will seek evidence that the local authority has carried out a meaningful assessment of the family and the conclusions of the assessment. Where the local authority has not been able to obtain agreement to work with the family, the local authority will need to produce evidence of any attempts to obtain agreement from the parents. Refusal to cooperate with an assessment will not by itself justify the making of an EPO if other options can be employed and it is reasonable and safe to do so.

The principles in *Re L (A Child)* [2007] above raise an important question as to whether a child should be removed before the appointment of an FCA. Following the review of the child care proceedings system in England and Wales, reforms to s. 31 CA89 proceedings were brought into effect in April 2008 by three key documents: Practice Direction 12A: Public law proceedings guide to case management (April 2010); the Children Act 1989 Guidance and Regulations, Volume 1: Court Orders in England; and the Children Act 1989 Guidance and Regulations, Volume 1: Court Orders (Wales) in Wales. The guidance states that where possible the FCA should meet with the child, where age-appropriate, and with other parties in advance of the first appointment.

On-the-spot question

What are the challenges for the local authority in establishing whether '*there is clear established evidence of immediate risk of really serious harm or imminent danger, which cannot be reduced without removal of the child*'?

> ### PRACTICE FOCUS
>
> Returning to the case study of Nancy and Jasper (see page 13) (applying the principles in *Re L (A Child)* [2007] above), the local authority has made a decision to make an application for a care order in respect of Jasper and intend to place Jasper in foster care when Nancy goes into hospital. Nancy is opposed to this, but feels she does not have any choice as she needs urgent treatment in hospital. Nancy has sought legal advice and her solicitor has advised the local authority that Nancy is not agreeable to the making of a care order and seeks the immediate return of Jasper to her care following her discharge from hospital. There are further issues raised in terms of Nancy's vulnerability and the possible need to involve the official solicitor at some stage to represent Nancy due to the difficulties in obtaining instructions from Nancy as her speech is deteriorating and her concentration is limited due to her worsening physical health and emotional wellbeing.
>
> Applying the principles in *Re L*, what will you need to consider in your statement and care plan for the court?

Alternative ways of handling an emergency: s. 20 CA89

Accommodation, or rather where the child is going to remain living and with whom, whilst an assessment is being undertaken is perhaps one of the most pressing issues when the local authority is dealing with an emergency situation. The decision as to whether a child should remain living at home or be '*looked after*' for a period will be based on an assessment of risk to the child. In applying the no order principle, the least restrictive option is for the child to remain living at home whilst an assessment is undertaken. In some circumstances, it may be appropriate for the child to remain living at home and the adult who presents the risk could be required to leave the home. The court has the power to make an exclusion requirement to an EPO (s. 44A CA89): where there is reasonable cause to believe that, if the relevant person is excluded from the child's home, the child will not be likely to suffer signficant harm or the local authority's s. 47 enquiries will not be threatened; there is someone else living there who is able and willing to give the child the care he or she needs; the person who will care for the child consents to the order being made. The court can attach the exclusion requirement where the conditions are met, requiring the named individual to leave the home. The court can accept a formal undertaking from the named person to leave and stay away from the home; alternatively the court can attach a power of arrest to the order.

There is an obvious tension here as the exclusion requirement is attached to an EPO for which the court has to be satisfied that the child is likely to suffer significant harm if he or she is not removed, but in the same application evidence must be provided to say that the child will not suffer harm or need to be removed from the home if the excluded person is removed. Evidence will clearly need to be presented in two parts: first, the criteria for the making of an EPO will need to be met before seeking the court's permission to consider the least restrictive option for the child, which is to require the person who presents the risk to leave. There are clearly practice issues here: the local authority may not be in a position at this stage to know who presents a greater risk to the child, and whether the removal of one person will ensure the child is safe. The very nature of an application for an EPO, as we have seen above, is where there is imminent risk of really serious harm and therefore a decision to leave the child at home in these circumstances requires careful consideration and a strategy discussion with the police before an application is made. A child may be at imminent risk of really serious harm, but agreement in some situations can be reached with the parents to have the child looked after for a short period of time whilst an assessment is undertaken.

If the initial assessment indicates the child should be looked after for a short period outside of the family home, and there are no other relatives/friends who are able to fulfil this role, providing the person with parental responsibility for the child consents, the local authority can provide accommodation (s. 20 CA89). A looked after child may either be a child who is subject to a care order and the local authority has parental responsibility, or a child who is *accommodated* and parents retain parental responsibility. Although the route into being a looked after child may be significantly different, during the period they are looked after they will be entitled to regular reviews and in both sets of circumstances be visited by a social worker.

The duty to accommodate is enshrined in CA89:

20

(1) Every local authority shall provide accommodation for any child in need within their area who appears to them to require accommodation as a result of—

(a) there being no person who has parental responsibility for him;

(b) his being lost or having been abandoned;

(c) or the person who has been caring for him being prevented (whether or not permanently, and for whatever reason) from providing him with suitable accommodation or care.

CA89

Initially, an assessment must be made as to whether providing accommodation is the most appropriate response to the child's needs, and whether any alternative services could and should be provided.

> Quotation from a parent: 'It is your plan not a plan that I agree with, but I have no choice, I either agree to voluntary care or you will take the kids anyway.'
>
> Clearly, the parent is not agreeing to her children being accommodated under s. 20 CA89 – there is no real consent.

This account from a parent highlighted two important issues from a recent research study. Firstly, parents' representatives, as in this example, did not challenge even when decisions were being made which the parents did not agree to. Secondly, the use of s. 20 accommodation in nearly all cases at some point in the case trajectory was viewed by professionals as a light touch, and this in particular was not challenged by advocates who, despite no clear consent from parents, were of the opinion that the contract was voluntary albeit under duress as the alternative was the local authority applying for a care order. As one solicitor said to a mother, 'you have to agree, you have no choice here, if you don't agree they will apply for care orders on all your children and you will have no say' (Holt et al., 2013).

Given the dominant role of law within the UK with respect to child protection, local authorities will have to find some way of managing the new administrative demands of the *PLO* (MoJ, 2008), but this will not necessarily result in improved or more effective relationships with parents. For example, under the *PLO*, it is entirely possible that significantly more use will be made of s. 20 CA89 agreements, as we have seen above.

Accommodating a child under s. 20 CA89 may be a positive move where this constitutes a safe and consensual approach to supporting families. However, in cases where the threshold criteria are met for an order under s. 31 CA89 and s. 20 is used to simply 'buy' the local authority more time (while the local authority completes the assessment work required to lodge an application to the courts under s. 31), then a number of problems are possible. This use of s. 20 will simply shift the locus of 'delay' to a point pre-proceedings (cf. McKeigue and Beckett, 2008). In addition, safeguards for both children and parents in this context may be weakened – for parents, the importance of access to independent legal representation may not be so evident. Foster placements under s. 20 are not scrutinized by the courts, nor are plans for children. In the context of cases that are likely to progress to an application to the court under s. 31, then the problems for partnership working are clear – parents may feel that they have not been given adequate support to understand or challenge the local authority's plans at an early point.

Similar arguments apply to the planned increase in use of family group conferences (FGCs) under the *PLO*. Shifting decision-making away from courts and into the mediated space of family and friends networks can be seen in many respects as very positive for all stakeholders. However, this shift is based on rather limited evidence of the effectiveness of the FGC model (Brown, 2003). As discussed, decision-making in such informal spaces is not subject to independent or external legal scrutiny – an independent chair is advised but not always appointed (Holt and Kelly, 2012b). The role of the court in child protection cases serves not only to ensure justice for children and parents, but also to hold the local authority accountable for its actions. This latter point is important because, as Cathy Ashley (chief executive of the Family Rights Group (FRG)) has cautioned, there is the distinct possibility that the necessary development of the FGC model will get 'lost in the shortcuts' as resources are increasingly focused on achieving the administrative demands of public law cases (Ashley, 2008).

There is some debate about the ideological underpinnings of current government enthusiasm for the FGC – this may have less to do with empowering parents and the extended family network and more to do with 'policy-makers seeking to reduce the bill for looked after children' (Welbourne, 2008:5).

There are circumstances where accommodating a child under s. 20 is not appropriate. A child, for example, who has no one with parental responsibility will not achieve this by s. 20(1)(a) CA89. The local authority would need to consider applying for a care order as this is the only route available to the local authority if it wishes to obtain parental responsibility for a child. The CA89 provides for a wide interpretation of eligibility and the word '*shall*' rather than must and the scope of defining a child in need will inevitably be driven by resource implications. The task of the social worker is to focus on a needs-led assessment, clearly identifying the child's needs and the resources required to meet that child's needs.

Importantly, the local authority has a specific duty in respect of young people aged 16 and 17 (s. 20(3) CA89) where '*his welfare is likely to be seriously prejudiced*' if he or she is not accommodated. Whilst not every 16 and 17-year-old will fall under the definition of a child in need, *R (M) v Hammersmith and Fulham* [2006], where a young person is '*in need*' the onus is not placed with the young person to request services which meet their needs: this falls appropriately on the local authority. Section 20(4) CA89 gives local authorities the power to accommodate a child even where there is no duty to do so.

Diverting cases away from court with the use of s. 20 CA89 to accommodate a child may appear consistent with the principle of partnership working under the CA89 in achieving consensual solutions, but the parents may not have the opportunity to challenge the local authority and indeed may agree to accommodation rather than face the risk of a care order being made. It is a concern that, in an attempt to either divert or resolve cases without judicial oversight, the evidence may never be properly challenged.

Accommodating a child under s. 20 should never be regarded as a *light touch*. Separating children from their parents must always be carefully considered and appropriate safeguards put in place to ensure both children and their families know their legal rights.

On-the-spot question	What advice would you give to parents to ensure they completely understand the full implications of requesting or agreeing to accommodation?

Summary

The challenge for all professionals involved in child protection is to improve decision-making in a timely manner with an obligation to provide better access to justice for children (Judiciary of England and Wales, 2012:4)

The final report of the *Family Justice Review* (MoJ, 2011a) and the Family Justice Modernisation Programme (Judiciary of England and

Wales, 2012) set in train a system that is quicker, simpler, more cost-effective and fairer, whilst continuing to protect children from risk of harm. Pivotal to achieving this aim is to ensure children remain the focus and are not lost amongst the competing needs and demands of adults. Parents and carers are clearly important and must be involved in the process, but decisions must be taken to protect children from harm at the earliest opportunity.

Alternative ways of dealing with an emergency are important, but we must ensure they meet the needs of children. Diverting cases away from court with the use of s. 20 CA89 to accommodate a child may appear consistent with the principle of partnership working under the CA89 in achieving consensual solutions, but the parents may not have the opportunity to challenge the local authority and indeed may agree to accommodation rather than face the risk of a care order being made. Importantly, if used to either divert or resolve cases without judicial oversight the evidence may never be properly challenged and this may introduce additional delay for children. A recent study undertaken by Kim Holt et al. (2013) found that in nearly all cases children had at some stage been accommodated under s. 20 and this had built in delay to the permanency planning for these children.

Here, we are reminded of the work of Packman et al. (1986) that pre-dated the CA89, but nevertheless raised questions about the voluntary accommodation of children in the context of child protection practice. Whilst there may be good reasons for local authorities to accommodate children under s. 20 CA89, there is a need to regularly review these placements to ensure they continue to meet the needs of the child.

Further reading

Ferguson, H (2010) 'Walks, home visits and atmospheres: risk and the everyday practices and mobilities of social work and child protection' 40(4) *British Journal of Social Work* 1100–17. This paper highlights the importance of place in social work assessments and draws upon research to examine what Ferguson refers to as practice risks.

Holt, K E, N Kelly, P Doherty and K Broadhurst (2013) 'Access to justice for families? Legal advocacy for parents where children are on the "edge of care": an English case study' 35(2) *Journal of Social Welfare and Family Law* 163–77. This paper draws on data from an English case study that examines the tensions of achieving justice for families where children are on the edge of care.

Lutman, E and E Farmer (2013) 'What contributes to outcomes for neglected children who are reunified with their parents? Findings from a five-year follow-up study' 43(3) *British Journal of Social Work* 559–78. There has been to date relatively little research undertaken on neglect – in essence neglect has been neglected. This study provides an important insight into the effects of neglect on children.

4

CARE AND SUPERVISION

What do we mean by the threshold criteria and how are they applied?

Historically, individuals have sought to resolve their disputes by turning to the courts – primarily to have an arbitrator to listen to their case and to obtain damages for any loss suffered; alternatively, to be able to formally defend any action taken against an individual before a decision is made. Civil and criminal law are significantly different in terms of their aims and procedures. Civil law concerns the relationship between individuals and individuals and corporations – examples of civil law are contract, employment, tort or family law. The evidential burden of proof is different to criminal law. In civil law the applicant only has to satisfy the court on the balance of probabilities for a decision to be found in their favour, whilst in a criminal court where an individual's liberty may be at stake the evidential burden is considerably higher and the applicant (the state) has to prove all elements of the offence, satisfying the court beyond reasonable doubt. In criminal law the relationship is clearly different in so far as it is the state taking action against an individual.

Public child care law is somewhat of an anomaly – although the evidential burden is the same as civil law – it is dealt with as a public law matter as the state is intervening in family life. It is a contentious issue that to remove a child requires the applicant local authority to satisfy to

→ **KEY CASE ANALYSIS** ←

Re B (Care Proceedings: Standard of Proof) [2008] *in particular per Baroness Hale at paras 70 and 72*

The facts of the case involved emotional harm and violence affecting four children and allegations of sexual abuse made by one child. Some had hoped and many feared that the House of Lords would reduce the standard of proof in children's cases, altering the threshold to be crossed based on a new lower test of *real possibility*. The House of Lords rejected this appeal, retaining the standard of proof as the balance of probabilities.

The threshold criteria means the test which must be satisfied before the court can make either a care or supervision order in favour of the local authority. It is essentially the first hurdle, but if we examine the wording of the threshold criteria below and we apply the evidential burden of proof on the balance of possibilities, we can see there is considerable margin for interpretation.

the court only the lower burden of proof, the threshold criteria that the child has suffered or is likely to suffer significant harm.

Care or supervision: how do you decide?

Establishing the threshold criteria for the making of an order is merely the starting point. More important is deciding which order or combination of orders to apply for. The decision regarding what order/combination of orders to apply for will be dependent upon the welfare of the child and again reference should be made to the welfare checklist (see Chapter 1 page 9).

Care orders

The decision to apply for a care order rests with the local authority. The court may be concerned about the welfare of a child when resolving a private matter as with divorce proceedings. The court may take the view that the threshold criteria are satisfied and the child should be made the subject of a care order. The court is limited in terms of what action it can take – the court can order a report under s. 37 CA89 and support it with the making of an interim care order, but, if the local authority conducts its own enquiries and concludes the making of a care order would not prioritize the welfare of the child, the court can do nothing. The ordering of a s. 37 report signals to the local authority that the court is inviting the local authority to consider making an application for a care order. This issue was debated in the Court of Appeal decision in *Nottingham County Council v P* [2008]. In the Nottingham case the local authority refused to apply for a care order, instead seeking to use a prohibited steps order that the Court of Appeal believed to be misconceived. Nevertheless, the court could do nothing if the local authority refused to apply for a care order.

Where a local authority decides to make an application for a care order or a supervision order:

31

(2) a court may only make a care order or supervision order if it is satisfied—
   (a) that the child concerned is suffering, or is likely to suffer, significant harm; and
   (b) that the harm, or likelihood of harm, is attributable to—

    (i) the care given to the child, or likely to be given to him if the order were not made, not being what it would be reasonable to expect a parent to give to him; or

    (ii) the child's being beyond parental control.

CA89

'Harm' is defined as '*ill-treatment or the impairment of health or development including, for example, impairment suffered from seeing or hearing the ill-treatment of another*'; 'ill-treatment' includes sexual abuse and forms of ill-treatment which are not physical; 'health' means physical or mental health; and 'development' means physical, intellectual, emotional, social or behavioural development (s. 31(9) CA89).

In order for the threshold to be crossed, the conditions set out in paras (a) and (b) above must be affirmatively established to the satisfaction of the court. The legal burden of establishing the existence of these conditions rests on the applicant for a care order as was decided in *Re H and Others (Minors)* [1995]. The standard of proof to be applied when establishing the threshold is the civil standard, that is the simple balance of probabilities (*Re B (Minors) (Sexual Abuse: Standard of Proof)* [2008]).

It is important to remember that the task of the court is to decide on the evidence before it and the court can and does depart from the view of expert evidence provided sound reasons are given for doing so, as per Ward LJ in *Re B (Care: Expert Witnesses)* [1996].

The right of appeal is a complex issue and falls outside the scope of this book, but it is important to note that an appeal against a court decision in a lower court must be approved by either the judge dealing with the matter in the lower court, or if not, an application will need to be made to a higher court for approval that the case is suitable for a review of the decision. It is not always the case that applications for appeal are successful, as in the case of *Re L (Children)* [2011] where Thorpe LJ dismissed the appeal.

An application for care/supervision proceedings should normally start in the Family Proceedings Court unless there are other proceedings already ongoing in a higher court – if so, the matter will be transferred to either the county court or High Court where the ongoing matter is being dealt with. An application can be made by a party in the proceedings to transfer the case on the basis of gravity, complexity or the likely length of the case at the final hearing. A case should be dealt with by an appropriate court with the level of expertise and time to deal with the matter. If a case involves complex legal arguments and evidence, much of which is disputed or likely to be disputed, the case should be transferred at the earliest opportunity to avoid a delay in the decision-making for the child. Any person with parental responsibility will automatically be made a party to the proceedings and invited to attend court with legal representation. Persons with parental responsibility will receive and be able to contribute to the evidence shared within the proceedings.

The child is always made a party to the proceedings and is represented by an FCA from Cafcass and a solicitor. Involvement of the child in the court proceedings will be dependent upon his or her age and level of understanding. It is usual practice for the FCA to make an assessment and to give instructions to the solicitor appointed by the FCA. However, if a child is of an age and has the capacity to dissent from the view of the FCA, the child can instruct the instructing solicitor to represent his or her own views and not the views of the FCA and the court will need to be notified of this situation. The court can hear directly from the child within the proceedings where evidence is crucial to deciding a case, but this needs to be carefully managed and a video link should be used to afford protection to the child. We are reminded of the Court of Appeal guidance in *LM v Medway Council and RM and YM* [2007] that is it *undesirable* for a child to attend court and there needs to be justification before this course of action is taken. A child may wish to talk to the judge who is dealing with the case and, if this is agreed by all the parties, it can be facilitated by the court.

The person with whom the child was living at the time the application was made is entitled to receive notice of the proceedings and attend court regardless of whether that person has parental responsibility. The court will hear applications for parties to be joined in the proceedings and the court can, where appropriate, join relevant people who have something different to contribute to the proceedings. Relatives may put themselves forward to care for the child rather than have the child living outside of the wider family and may seek to apply for a private law order under s. 8 CA89. A relative may during care proceedings put themselves forward to be assessed by the local authority with a view to applying for a residence order under s. 8 CA89. The local authority cannot apply for a s. 8 order as this is a private law order, but it can support a relative applying for a residence order and this may be the outcome of care proceedings possibly bolstered by the making of a supervision order for a limited period of time to provide a statutory level of involvement with the family to ensure the plan continues to safeguard and promote the welfare of the child.

Whilst there is considerable pressure to conclude cases in a timely manner (House of Commons Justice Committee, 2012: para. 43), complex cases do take time to resolve, particularly where there is complex and conflicting medical evidence or where the Official Solicitor has to be appointed where a party is not able to give instructions because they are assessed as not having the capacity to do so. In the interim an order can be made which gives the local authority shared parental responsibility with the parent for the child. Before making an interim care order the court has to be satisfied that the threshold criteria in s. 31(2) CA89 are met and the child requires interim protection as was decided in *Re K and H* [2006]. A court may make directions during the interim period for further assessment work to be undertaken to inform the court at the final stage.

Supervision orders

The criteria for a supervision order are exactly the same as with an application for a care order above. The local authority must satisfy the threshold criteria as outlined in Chapter 1 (see page 9). The question for the local authority is, if the threshold criteria as outlined above are met, how will the making of a supervision order be better for the child than the making of no order?

It must be the case that the local authority is concerned about the welfare of the child otherwise it would not be making an application in the first instance, so it must be assumed the risk is not so high that it warrants the child being removed from the home. The making of a supervision order does not confer parental responsibility to the local authority so the parents retain full parental responsibility. The making of a supervision order does allow the local authority to retain a statutory role in terms of visiting the child and being informed of any changes in respect of the child. The role is to advise, assist and befriend the child (s. 35(1)(a) CA89). The duration of the order is significantly different to that of a care order. A care order is made until the child reaches 18 unless the court, following an application by either the local authority or the parent, discharges the order, or if the court makes a residence order or adoption order which automatically discharges the care order. In contrast the making of a supervision order lasts for 12 months. The order may be extended up to a maximum of three years, but this must be done by an application to extend.

The risk of the local authority in applying for a supervision order is that the court upon receiving this application may decide the risk is too high and upon hearing all the evidence may decide to make a care order, as was the case in *Re D (Minor) (Care or Supervision Order)* [1993]. Alternatively, the local authority may seek a care order but the case may be decided by the making of a supervision order. The making of a super-vision order is not to be treated lightly as parents' failure to comply with the order could be used by the local authority to make a fresh applica-tion for a care order, an important statement made by the Court of Appeal in *Re O (A Child) (Supervision Order: Future Harm)* [2001].

On-the-spot questions	1 In what circumstances would you consider seeking a supervision order as opposed to a care order? 2 Applying the no order principle, would it be possible to achieve the same outcome for the child with no order and agreeing a plan with the child and family?

Care planning

An application for a care or supervision order must be supported with a care plan. The court will need to be satisfied that the local authority has considered the welfare of the child and applied the welfare checklist in Chapter 1 (page 9) when considering the plan for the child should the court make a care order. The care plan must be detailed and the local authority must satisfy the court that detailed plans including contact between the child and family during the period the order is in force have been fully considered.

The court cannot make a care order without being satisfied that the care plan is a realistic one for the child (s. 31(3A) CA89), which the local authority has a statutory duty to produce and review (s. 31A CA89). A care plan is required for each child as their individual needs, wishes and feelings will be specific to them. The details of the care plan for a sibling group must never be migrated from the previous plan; every child is unique and this must be reflected in a considered care plan for each child. The care plan is the document that is often challenged by parent's legal representatives and the court. The priority must be to identify the needs of the child and this must take precedence over resource implica-tions for the local authority. The court is not interested in the resource/financial constraints on the local authority: the priority for the court is ensuring that the welfare of a particular child is being properly considered and a sensible and coherent plan is in place for the child. The court has rather controversially attempted to keep track of care planning

Bury MBC v D [2009]

In *Bury MBC v D*, Mumby J was concerned with the fairness of local authority decision-making *after* a care order had been made. Parents complained that the local authority had, in effect, substituted an entirely new care plan, involving removal of their children, without involving them properly in the process.

Mumby J agreed. Commenting on what Article 8 required (at para. 43), he said: 'A local authority, even if clothed with the authority of a care order, is not entitled to make significant changes in the care plan, or to change the arrangements under which the children are living, let alone to remove the children from home if they are living with their parents, without properly involving the parents in the decision-making process and without giving the parents a proper opportunity to make their case before a decision is made.'

Furthermore (at para. 59): 'Parents who find themselves involved in cases such as this are often themselves vulnerable, sometimes very vulnerable; they may suffer from physical or mental disabilities or be educationally, economically or socially disadvantaged. They are often ill equipped to cope with those whom they understandably see as "them".'

for children following the making of a care order due to being concerned about the prospects of the plan being delivered being undermined by resource factors.

The concern raised by Munby J above is echoed by Nagalro below, who highlights that in a climate of austerity, and with the impact of comprehensive spending reviews on local authorities, ensuring the interests of children are prioritized in care plans may not be of central importance alongside other competing demands.

Court scrutiny of care plans is essential to ensure the local authority assessment and planning is sound. Vulnerable children will suffer miscarriages of justice if their cases receive only a cursory glance. The government shows a touching faith in local authorities to be all things to all children when evidence shows their performance is extremely variable. The interests of children are often at odds with the financial interests of local authorities ...

Nagalro, 2012

The judicial scrutiny of local authority care plans when an application for a care order is made is crucially important, but, with an increasing focus on cases being diverted away from court at the pre-proceedings stage, it raises an important question of who independently scrutinizes the care plan when a case is not before a court. Whilst the role of the independent reviewing officer (IRO) should be crucial in this regard, the independent nature of the role has been questioned when the IRO is employed by the same local authority (Holt et al., 2013). The question is raised that, if the IRO cannot affectively independently scrutinize the care plan, consideration must be given to the availability of advocacy for parents and children.

Merely because a decision is taken administratively rather than by a court is not of itself any reason why a parent or child should not be adequately represented. If the administrative decision-maker is to comply with the ECHR, he or she must not merely have regard to the parent's or the child's rights under Article 8, the decision-maker must also make sure that their interests are appropriately represented. Furthermore, the decision-maker must ensure that the child's voice and the parent's voice are heard.

> **PRACTICE FOCUS**
>
> Returning to the case study of Jasper and Nancy (see page 13), the local authority made an application for a care order that was agreed by the court. The local authority plan is to accommodate Jasper for an anticipated period of four weeks whilst Nancy is in hospital, but to return Jasper to the care of Nancy following her discharge from hospital, providing she is able to continue to care for Jasper with the support from her care staff.
>
> • Considering *Bury MBC v D* (above). How can you ensure you involve Nancy properly in the process of reviewing the care plan?
> • What level of contact and with whom will you provide to Jasper whilst Nancy is in hospital?

Statutory reviews

The absence of any system for bringing local authorities to account for the failure to adhere to care plans was causing concern amongst members of the judiciary. The initial decision of the Court of Appeal in *Re*

W (Care Plan) [2001] to track cases, either by delaying the making of a final care order, or setting milestones for the local authority following the making of a final care order, was met with approval. However, this position was not replicated when the government responded to the overturning of that decision by the House of Lords in *Re S (Minors) (Care Order: Implementation of Care Plan); Re W (Minors) (Care Order: Adequacy of Care Plan)* [2002] by introducing the legal requirement for an IRO to be appointed for each looked after child. The Court of Appeal decision (now referred to as *Re S and Re W*) was perceived as the court appointing itself as the monitor of the local authority and its responsibilities towards children in local authority care. The House of Lords confirmed that it was not for the court to take on that role; legislation was needed to create a formal monitoring of the duties held by the local authority.

An amendment to s. 26 of the CA89 (made by the Adoption and Children Act 2002) created the **statutory review**: a statutory duty to appoint an IRO to participate in case reviews, monitor the local authority's performance in reviews and to consider whether it would be appropriate to refer cases to Cafcass.

Whilst it is undoubtedly the case that there are looked after children whose rights have been breached by the actions (or inactions) of local authorities, it could be possible that these breaches have been resolved internally in the local authority without the IRO having to refer to Cafcass. Whilst the rate of referral to Cafcass is not the only, or even most important, measure of the success or failure of the IRO scheme, there is little evidence that dispute resolution processes in many authorities have been used or, indeed, that such processes even exist in some authorities. Where decision-making occurs without the oversight of the court, the problem of not involving or hearing children may be compounded by the fact that care plans may have no effective independent scrutiny. *Re S v Rochdale* [2008] illustrates that, although procedures do exist to ensure independent and effective review, these sometimes fail. Given the task of the family justice system to deal with an increasing number of cases outside of the court, the need for good representation for all parties is crucial to ensure effective scrutiny of such important decisions (Masson, 2008).

Statutory reviews for looked after children

Looked after children, regardless of their route into accommodation provided by the local authority are required to have regular reviews.

Once a care order is made, the responsibility for the child lies with the local authority, which must take responsibility as part of its corporate parenting role to review every child who is looked after. Similarly, children who are accommodated under s. 20 CA89 with parental agreement are required to have regular reviews whilst they remain looked after by the local authority.

The appointment of the IRO, a qualified and experienced social worker who is independent to the case, is pivotal in ensuring that every looked after child is kept under review. The role and function of the IRO is to be found in the Review of Children's Cases (Amendment) (England) Regulations 2004 and the Independent Reviewing Officers Guidance 2004, which is issued under s. 7 Local Authority Social Services Act 1970 and must be followed. There is debate as to the independence of the IRO when the role remains located within the local authority and the IRO is effectively employed by the local authority for whom they are required to be independent (Broadhurst and Holt, 2010).

The first review for the child must be held within four weeks of the child first becoming looked after, then within three months and thereafter every six months. The role of the IRO is to ensure reviews are held within the timescales above and, where appropriate to do so, to bring forward a review. The IRO reviews pathway plans for young people aged 16 and above who remain looked after by the local authority. The IRO must ensure the child is the focus of the review and that the voice of the child is heard, which may involve the IRO meeting the child outside of the review where it is appropriate to do so.

The review should remain child-focused and family-centred and the venue for the review should be accessible to all participants. Consideration needs to be given as to who should contribute to the review and who should attend, as these may be different depending on the situation and circumstances of each child.

Importantly, the review should review the care plan to ensure that it is being adhered to and appropriate resources identified and agreed to ensure the plan continues to be effective and current. A plan may need to be revised as the child's needs change, and this should be discussed and agreed at the review with contingency plans built into the review. As stated above, the IRO can effectively challenge the local authority for failure to carry out an effective and agreed plan and ultimately can refer the matter to court or Cafcass. This may prompt local authorities to carefully consider their corporate parenting duties in relation to looked after children to avoid a complaint and possible external challenge to decision-making within the local authority.

Contact

Contact is an important aspect of the care plan and the court must consider contact arrangements as part of the care plan before the making of a care order (s. 34(11) CA89). Contact is a wide concept and is dealt with essentially under s. 8 and s. 34 CA89. Contact disputes that arise from the breakdown of a relationship and are dealt with in private law proceedings are the focus of s. 8, which extends beyond the scope of this book. The focus here will be on contact arrangements, when children are looked after by the local authority either following the making of a care order by the court or by agreement with the parents.

Parental contact with children in care is dealt with in s. 34 CA89 that states:

34

(1) Where a child is in the care of a local authority, the authority shall (subject to the provisions of this section) allow the child reasonable contact with—
    (a) his parents;
    (b) any guardian or special guardian; any person who by virtue of section 4A has parental responsibility for him;
    (c) where there was a residence order in force with respect to the child immediately before the care order was made, the person in whose favour the order was made; and
    (d) where, immediately before the care order was made, a person had care of the child by virtue of an order made in the exercise of the High Court's inherent jurisdiction with respect to children, that person.

CA89

In respect of children in care, there is a presumption of reasonable contact for parents, unless there are cogent reasons to refuse contact. What is reasonable will be determined by the specifics of each individual case and an evaluation of all the circumstances of the child.

The important issue for practitioners is to ensure contact arrangements are in the best interests of the child. It is always a useful starting point to consider the welfare checklist in s. 1(3) CA89 to assess what level of contact should be organized, with whom and whether contact is direct/indirect or a combination of both. The child's wishes and feelings are crucial and must underpin the social work assessment – it is all too easy to focus on the adult agendas and not to give due weight to the voice of the child. The local authority has a statutory duty to all looked after children to promote contact between a child and his or her parents, anyone with parental responsibility for the child, relative, friend, or anyone else connected with the child unless it is not practicable or consistent with the welfare of the child (para. 15, schedule 2 CA89).

It is important that the child retains contact with significant people whilst accommodated by the local authority. The local authority must ensure wherever possible that the child enjoys the same level of contact with people who are important and significant in the child's life.

In certain situations the local authority must act to refuse contact provided that it is a reasonable exercise of its discretion. However, the local authority must not refuse contact to a person who has a statutory right to reasonable contact. The local authority must seek an order from the court if it intends to refuse contact. The local authority must make an application to the court and the court must be satisfied there is a probable need to terminate contact, which is foreseeable and not too remote, before making an order under s. 34(4) CA89 which authorizes the local authority to refuse contact between a named person and the child. This important point was debated prior to the Court of Appeal's decision in *Re T (Termination of Contact: Discharge of Order)* [1997].

Summary

The issues faced by the family justice system are complex, requiring professional skill and judgment when families turn to it in times of great stress and when they are in crisis (*Family Justice Review*, MoJ, 2011a).

On 30 November 2011, the DfE published its annual update on Characteristics of Children in Need in England. The statistics show a rise in the number of children in need in England. There were 382,400 children in need at 31 March 2011, with a total of 735,500 episodes of need throughout the year. The number of children subject to a s. 47 investigation which started in the 2010–2011 year was 111,700. Nationally, the number of care cases also continues to rise with 65,520 looked after children at 31 March 2011, an increase of 2 per cent from 2010 and an increase of 9 per cent since 2007.

In 2011, following the tragic death of Peter Connelly and the increased number of care order applications, the average case duration was 57 weeks, rising to 61 weeks in the county court and High Court. In the modernizing family justice programme the train is set to reduce the timescale for care applications to be completed within 26 weeks. Primary legislation is currently before the House of Lords and the Crime and Courts Bill, creating the single family court, and pre-legislative scrutiny is taking place of what will become the Children and Families Bill which will address the government's welfare proposals in both public and private law cases and create further challenges for both families and professionals involved in the family justice system.

The decision to remove a child from the care of his or her parents and place that child in the care of the local authority is acknowledged as being incredibly difficult – relying on professional skill and judgment (Maclean and Kurczewski, 2011; Masson, 2011). Moreover, the *Family Justice Review* (MoJ, 2011a) highlights the need to have the most experienced and skilled professionals involved in these very difficult decisions.

The initiation of care proceedings often results in complete breakdown of relationships between the local authority and parents (Woodhouse, 1995; Holland and Scourfield, 2004). The level of conflict between parents and the state stems from discordance between the parents' view of the causes for concern and those of the state, as well as disagreement about the need for compulsory removal of children (Harwin, 1992; Freeman and Hunt, 1998; Brophy, 2006). Pam Freeman and Joan Hunt (1998) found that there was little agreement between parents and professionals about the grounds for concern and parents were extremely negative about the help offered from the local authority.

We know from the evidence base that overstretched local authorities find it hard to reach families who are seeking support as they weed out far more contacts and referrals than they open for initial assessment and in some cases families will be filtered out, when in fact, they are in urgent need of help (Gibbons et al., 1995; Broadhurst, Wastell et al., 2009).

Research undertaken in two local authorities by Broadhurst et al. (2011) highlighted the number of self-referrals or family referrals that were disproportionately filtered out, making direct approaches for help on the part of families difficult. This is an important observation as research has also found parents approach the local authority with concerns about children as a last resort (Broadhurst, 2007).

Further reading

Masson, J (2011b) 'Reforming care proceedings: a socio-legal perspective' in M Thorpe and W Tyzack (eds), *Dear David: A Memo to the Norgrove Committee from the Dartington Conference 2011*; 79–87. This chapter draws on research examining care proceedings from a socio-legal perspective.

Morris, K (2012) 'Thinking family? the complexities for family engagement in care and protection' 42(5) *British Journal of Social Work* 906–20. The paper raises some of the questions for future developments in family engagement in care and protection.

Thoburn, J (2012) 'Achieving successful returns from care: what makes reunification work?' 42(5) *British Journal of Social Work* 995–97. A paper that probes an important issue on returning children home from care.

5

POLICIES, PROTOCOLS AND PROCEDURES: A WAY FORWARD POST-MUNRO

AT A GLANCE THIS CHAPTER COVERS:

- a way forward post-Munro
- the historical development of judicial protocols
- the *Public Law Outline* and pre-proceedings protocols
- decision-making

Nationally the number of care applications continues to rise at a time where already limited resources are being targeted within formal pre-proceedings protocols aimed at achieving consensual solutions wherever possible to avoid cases going to court. The impetus for attempting to divert some cases where appropriate and safe to do so away from court is desirable in achieving positive outcomes for children and reducing delay. However, despite the rhetoric of the need for more direct engagement with families, there appears no relief from the procedural and managerial processes set within a context of public sector cuts affecting all professionals tasked with protecting children. The issues faced by the family justice system are complex, requiring professional skill and judgment when families turn to it in times of great stress and when they are in crisis (*Family Justice Review*, MoJ, 2011a).

Significantly, care application demand has remained at a consistently high level. Between April and June 2012 Cafcass received a total of 2534 applications. This figure is 6.7 per cent higher when compared to the same period in the previous year. Applications received during April and May 2012 have been the highest ever recorded by Cafcass for these individual months, with the 972 applications received in May 2012 being the highest ever recorded for a single month (Cafcass, 2012). Both sets of figures are significant when we consider the family justice system because social workers, who are key professionals working within the system, need to support both children who are in need and on the edge of care and children and their families who enter the family justice system. Dealing with increasing volumes of work, with no matching increase in resources, whilst at the same time attempting to reduce delay in court will continue to present the family justice system and frontline practitioners with a real challenge (Masson, 2010).

Despite the seemingly robust legislative framework (that clearly aims to support the upbringing of children within their families), we continue to see a significant increase in the number of care proceedings, prompting commentators such as Karen Broadhurst and Kim Holt (2012) to acknowledge an unprecedented rise in the number of care proceedings which has consequences for all practitioners operating within the family justice system.

This emphasis on moving important decision-making within pre-proceedings protocols is highly complex and has implications for local authorities which are tasked with operating a quasi-judicial protocol alongside an increased regulatory framework, thus adding further procedural steps for an already overly regulated social work profession (Broadhurst et al., 2011).

The historical development of judicial protocols

The *Protocol for Judicial Case Management in Public Law Children Act Cases* (MoJ, 2003) and its associated Practice Direction [2003] 2 FLR 719 were launched in November 2003. The protocol was received amongst lawyers with a mixture of high hopes and extreme cynicism. Khan reported ambivalence towards the protocol amongst members of the legal profession with a number of practitioners claiming not to have read it. The varied response to the protocol may in part be explained by the lack of ownership of the protocol and resistance to change (Khan, 2006). The foreword to the protocol states that the average care case lasts for almost a year.

> This is a year in which the child is left uncertain as to his or her future, is often moved between several temporary care arrangements, and the family and the public agencies are left engaged in protracted and complex legal wrangling. We believe that it is essential that unnecessary delay is eliminated and that better outcomes for children and families are thereby achieved.
>
> *MOJ, 2003:i*

Whilst the rhetoric and aspirations to tackle 'drift' are laudable, there is no acknowledgment of how this is to be operationalized, with key professionals such as social workers already saddled with increasing regulation and bureaucracy and with no impending increase in resources to cope with the aspirations of policy-makers (White and Broadhurst, 2009).

The key principles underlying the Practice Direction (Care cases: judicial continuity and judicial case management) (appended to Practice Direction [2003] 2 FLR 719) focused on achieving judicial continuity; active case management; standardization of steps; and the establishment of a case management conference. The aspirations of the protocol in achieving good judicial case management in public law proceedings was ambitious in a context where there was no clear evidence of sanctions for non-compliance with the protocol (Khan, 2006). The aim was to achieve active case management and the judiciary was tasked with implementing standardized steps embedded in a system that would be performance-reviewed to ensure compliance in achieving swift resolutions to public law cases.

The historical development of judicial protocols for case management in public law child care cases can be described as procedural steps designed to deal with the increasing concern around delay and costs in public law child care proceedings. However, simply increasing regulation and procedure is unlikely to address significant obstacles that fundamentally rest with a system, and those who work within it, at overload (Holt and Kelly, 2012a).

Whilst acknowledging and recognizing the work already involved in this area, the protocol, Practice Direction and the *Thematic Review of the Protocol for Judicial Case Management in Public Law Children Act Cases* (JRT, 2005) highlighted several principal areas for serious concern with a prediction of an increase in the volume of cases anticipated to be dealt with by the court. Principally there was concern regarding the unnecessary delay caused by a range of factors, such as: poorly prepared applications; scarcity of judicial resources; families' lack of understanding of the process; the complexity of cases; and the need for better interagency working. A further barrier to the successful completion of cases in a timely manner is the capacity of court listings to allocate for a final hearing that can often result in a child waiting months for the matter to be resolved despite all the parties being in a position to proceed (Blacklaws and Lickorish Quinn, 2010). Whilst the scarcity of judicial resources is quite appropriately highlighted as a reason for change, merely attempting to reduce delay to solve one problem only places the additional burden on local authorities to deliver more effectively at a time when they are experiencing similar resource constraints (Blacklaws, 2009). Furthermore, a range of recommendations followed to underscore the aspirations of the protocol and this chapter will focus on those relevant to social work practice.

Local authorities were advised under the protocol that they should write in plain English to the family, giving the reasons for their application to court and providing the family with a copy of the interim care plan. There has been considerable debate about the quality of social work reports produced within court proceedings particularly when the report format is an electronic template that requires all fields to be completed. It is acknowledged that, whilst there are some very good reports produced, practice amongst social workers is variable (White and

Broadhurst, 2009). Increased workloads and the digitization of social work reports has led in recent years to a culture of social workers migrating information between documents. These technologies may meet the regulatory requirements of the individual organization but they often make little sense to families or other professionals (Wastell et al., 2010).

Moreover, the protocol recommended that local authorities should facilitate access to independent legal advice for families earlier in the process by providing contact details for local Children Panel solicitors. Local authorities do encourage families to seek independent legal advice (Broadhurst and Holt, 2010) but there is often a reluctance amongst families who are hard to reach to engage with legal help before a case goes to court (Broadhurst et al., 2011) and cuts to legal funding have further compounded this problem. In Jessiman et al.'s study in 2009 they noted the *PLO* (amongst other things) had not appeared to enhance parental capacity to benefit from legal advice at the pre-proceedings stage. Where parents had been involved with a local authority for some time, Jessiman et al. noted that they may be slow to access legal advice for a number of reasons, including their own vulnerability or limited capacity to understand the letter before proceedings, or their perception of legal representation as part of the system 'threatening' them and their families.

Furthermore, the protocol recommended that all safe and appropriate alternatives should be explored before court proceedings are started. In some cases this might include placement with other family members, or providing support through FGCs to discuss all aspects of the family situation.

There is no evidence to suggest that local authorities initiate proceedings unnecessarily – quite the reverse, all too often local authorities have been criticized by the courts for not bringing cases to court at an earlier stage (Munby, 2009). Social workers are tasked to divert cases from care proceedings where it is safe and desirable to do so: these procedures further reinforce the importance of coordinated, multi-agency planning involving families in that process and recommend that essential assessment work is completed before cases are brought before the courts, including consideration of kin. Pre-proceedings work should include the routine completion of a detailed assessment (MoJ, 2011a).

In addition, guidance and best practice on case preparation should be written up in one document and used by all local authorities. The review team emphasized the importance of local authorities following

> **KEY CASE ANALYSIS**

R (L and Others) v Manchester City Council [2001]

In *R (L and Others) v Manchester City Council* [2001], Manchester City Council's policy on payments to kinship carers was successfully challenged as a result of the local authority adopting a policy of paying less to relatives who were foster carers. This effectively prevented the continuation of a family placement and as a result the rights of the child under Article 8 ECHR were not respected. The action was taken against the local authority as a result of the decision made at the pre-proceedings stage to pay short-term kinship carers of looked after children significantly less than approved local authority foster carers. Although, once approved as long-term carers by the local authority, they were paid at the normal rate.

Munby J found the local authority policy to be both irrational and contrary to Article 8 of the ECHR. The impact of the judgment is that payments to kinship carers must be made on the same basis as local authority carers whether it is a short-term or long-term arrangement. Any difference should relate to the child's needs, the skills of the carer, or some other relevant factor that is used as a basis for an authority-wide policy. Despite the clear judgment from Munby J, there is evidence that kin are still being paid at a lower rate, notwithstanding the reliance placed upon kin to provide an alternative to care within the context of pre-proceedings.

In child protection practice it can be seen that the ECHR requires the state to engage in a most sensitive balancing exercise. The incorporation of the ECHR has implications for the way in which local authorities conduct themselves in performing their statutory role and for the allocation of their resources.

the statutory guidance to ensure cases are ready for proceedings before applications are made. Here we see evidence of an attempt to introduce further standardization and procedures to an already over-regulated profession. There is a belief by legislators and policy-makers that increased regulation that is understood at one level is translated into practice in a unified and consistent way. However, there is often a tension between policy ideals and the reality on the ground (Featherstone, Broadhurst et al., 2011).

The *Thematic Review* (JRT, 2005) recommended that case management in the courts should be improved. In part the problem has evolved

> ### ◤ PRACTICE FOCUS
>
> Returning to the case study of Jasper and Nancy (see page 13), Kathryn, who is one of Nancy's carers and who has known Jasper since birth, has discussed this imminent situation of Nancy going into hospital with her partner. Kathryn and her partner wish to be considered as an alternative to Jasper being accommodated with foster carers who are not known to him. Kathryn and her partner have also expressed a wish to be assessed as permanent carers for Jasper when Nancy is not able to continue to live at home.
> Nancy is fully in support of this plan.
>
> - What if anything can be done in the short term to allow Jasper to live with Kathryn and her partner whilst Nancy is in hospital?
> - Considering *R (L & Others)* (above) what consideration to payment will need to be given in the short term if a placement with Kathryn and her partner is considered? Kathryn and her partner are on a limited income.

due to an increased volume of work which members of the judiciary are required to navigate, the complexity of the cases involved which require skill and judgment and the importance of ensuring that families' rights under Articles 6 and 8 ECHR are supported and protected (Holt and Kelly, 2012a).

The case management conference was seen as pivotal in achieving the aims of the protocol. However, attempts to achieve swift case resolution have continued to be hampered by the overuse of experts and the non-availability of reports. There appeared to have been minimal challenge to the use of experts to assess individuals and relationships within the family when there was no obvious evidence requiring a high level of additional expertise. The reason cited is often the lack of experience of the social worker, but this is not sufficient reason for instructing an expert. A clear distinction is not being made between fact-finding (when the most technical experts are used) and disposal. Mental health experts are being used in the latter stage when an experienced social worker may be more suitable. Also, unnecessarily experienced experts are being used in cases where the evidence of the social worker should suffice (Masson, 2011a).

In an attempt to achieve the aspirations of the protocol, the review team considered whether further work should be undertaken to determine whether joint targets and funds could encourage closer working relation-ships, joint planning and shared priorities between the various agencies involved, a theme developed in the *Family Justice Review* (MoJ: 2011a).

The JRT commissioned a further review undertaken by Dr Julia Brophy (2006) to provide an evidence-based background to the work of the team in reviewing care proceedings and to provide further information on the process and nature of applications for care orders. Brophy identi-fied that most final hearings are not the dramatic and adversarial exam-ination of all evidence and cross-examination of parties and positions which a lay audience may envisage. This is because the real work has taken place over the preceding months in detailed assessments and negotiations (Brophy, 2006:83)

The *Public Law Outline*: taking practice forward?

This Practice Direction has the overriding objective of enabling the court to deal with cases justly, having regard to the welfare issues involved (MoJ, 2008:1).

The Practice Direction: Guide to case management in public law proceedings [2008] 2 FLR 668, more commonly referred to as the *PLO*, is a response to both the *Thematic Review* published by the JRT (2005) and the *Review of Child Care Proceedings in England and Wales* commis-sioned by the former Department for Constitutional Affairs (DCA, 2006a). The *PLO* replaced the *Protocol for Judicial Case Management* (MoJ, 2003) and required a re-ordering of the way care proceedings are instigated, structured and conducted. The *PLO* involves two stages: 'pre-proceedings' and 'post-instigation of proceedings'; in the latter the court process is reduced from six to four stages, each with explicit timescales attached to procedures, and the local authority is required to provide a detailed core assessment and care plan at the issuing of proceedings and first appointment hearing. In the pre-proceedings stage the aim is to maximize the possibility of resolving cases without proceedings and the *PLO* makes mandatory certain steps that are to be taken prior to proceed-ings being issued. These require the local authority to: carry out assess-ment work prior to the instigation of proceedings; identify and assess any possible alternative placements with relatives and friends; and explore all possible alternatives to instigating proceedings.

Should the local authority consider that proceedings are necessary (and not of such a nature that the welfare of the child requires immediate court protection), it must convene a meeting between the social worker and local authority legal advisor (a legal planning meeting) and a letter before proceedings must be sent to the parents. This letter must summarize concerns, state actions required to remedy those concerns, provide information on what the local authority has done to safeguard the children to date, and state what outcome would be likely if the concerns are not addressed. The letter before proceedings invites parents to a pre-proceedings meeting to be convened with the local authority legal advisor and social worker/s and must advise parents on how to obtain legal advice and representation at that meeting. Significantly, Jessiman et al.'s (2009) respondents (members of the legal profession and FCAs) noted that timescales between receiving the letter before proceedings and proceedings being issued may not be adequate to allow meaningful engagement with parents and, perhaps more fundamentally, the investment by the local authority in the pre-proceedings work may be perceived as an intention to proceed.

Whilst these procedures may have been in place in local authorities prior to the *PLO*, the letter before proceedings sent to the parents provides a more formal statement of the local authority position and clear information to parents that they have the right to legal representation at the pre-proceedings meeting. Whilst the intention of the *PLO* sounds convincing, in practice Masson (2008) expressed concerns that these developments were being established in a context of reduced legal funding in family work and raised serious concerns about fair access to justice.

Furthermore, Masson suggests that a two-tier system may emerge resulting in a local authority having a distinct advantage in terms of access to the most experienced legal advice and representation and parents in contrast finding it difficult to find an experienced representative. The public law fee level remains fixed at levels one and two (Legal Services Commission Fee Scheme Guidance, 2011 (MoJ, 2011a)) thus raising further concern that families may not have fair access to experienced legal representation at the important pre-proceedings stage. Unequal access to legal representation is likely to impact further on attempts to provide an integrated family justice system.

The *PLO* was initially revised in April 2010 in an attempt to reduce the bureaucratic burden of paperwork at the point of issue with the aim of prioritizing the timetable for the child. In practice the only change is how and when the documentation is presented. Although much of the documentation is not required to be filed with the application, it is required by the first appointment, five days later. The author, similarly to the view expressed by Blacklaws and Lickorish Quinn (2010), remains to be convinced this has made any significant difference to the volume of paperwork and bureaucracy.

Following the recommendations of the *Family Justice Review*, the government proposed legislation (MoJ and DfE, 2012:16, para. 55) to impose a statutory six-month time limit for the completion of care cases (in 2013 the average duration of a case from start to finish was 55 weeks). Where appropriate cases should be progressed more quickly, and only in *exceptional* cases where the best interests of the child are served and reasons for further delay are clear, an extension may be granted. This is reiterated in the third update on *The Family Justice Modernisation Programme* where Ryder J states:

> The single most important change that I recommend is the creation of standard and exceptional case tracks with guidance in the form of a pathway that describes how some cases can and should be completed within 26 weeks.
>
> *Judiciary of England and Wales, 2012:3*

This theme was further developed at a press conference on the modernization of family justice by Mr Justice Ryder at the Royal Courts of Justice on 31 July 2012:

> There is a clear recognition that a change of culture is required to root out unnecessary delay while maintaining the quality of the decisions we make. We have an obligation to provide better access to justice for children.
>
> *Judiciary of England and Wales, 2012:4*

The *Family Justice Review* (MoJ, 2011a; 2011b), and the subsequent Family Justice Modernisation Programme that began in 2012, set in train a programme of reform of the family justice system. Revisions to the *PLO* included in the Practice Direction 36C: Pilot scheme: care and supervision proceedings and other proceedings under Part 4 of the Children Act 1989 support the overriding objective to ensure proportionate use of resources within the timeframe for the child.

Furthermore, these changes reflect a significant focus and attention to ensuring that delays in decision-making in relation to care proceedings are kept to a minimum both within the pre-proceedings protocol and when a court is managing a case. It is evident that within this culture timescales for working with families are being reduced and more tightly defined (Holt et al., 2013). In all but the most exceptional cases a deadline of 26 weeks for resolving a dispute is imposed following the application for a care order (Practice Direction 36C 2013).

Central to achieving the aim of providing a cost-effective and fair system whilst continuing to protect children is the effective engagement of both parents and children at the pre-proceedings stage. Pivotal to ensuring that these aspirations are achieved is to provide representation of the highest quality, by professionals who have the knowledge and skills to undertake this vitally important work.

Thus, greater demands are made of local authorities with regard to assessment and family support. Documentation detailing discussions with families that provides evidence that voluntary, non-legal solutions have been sought in the first instance must now be filed with the court. Reflecting the *PLO*'s central concern with improving parental engagement, paras 3.24 and 3.32 of the revised CA89 guidance (DCSF, 2008) cite the utility of the family group conference in facilitating the engagement of friends and wider family at an early stage, with respect to substitute care. When cases are brought before the courts, increased responsibility is placed on professionals to ensure that parents understand court processes, and that intentions to initiate proceedings are explained to the child and parent using appropriate language and methods of communication. Assessment must take into account parents' capacities to instruct a legal representative. Effective parental engagement is also seen as providing the possibility of narrowing the issues brought before the courts, thus leading to swifter case resolution (Maclean and Eekelaar, 2010).

The impetus to attempt to resolve disputes within pre-proceedings protocols rather than the reliance on judicial decision-making is persuasive; engaging with families to achieve consensual solutions in an attempt to divert cases away from court is desirable in achieving positive outcomes for children and reducing delay. The *PLO* appeared to hold out the promise of a fairer process for families. Whilst the rhetoric of the *PLO* to provide consensual solutions within administrative rather than judicial decision-making processes may be laudable, there are tensions and dilemmas in relation to ensuring that the rights of parents and children are protected (Broadhurst and Holt, 2010).

The author questions whether the 'settlement culture' (agreeing matters to avoid a court hearing) that has been evident since the late 1980s (Davis, 1988) is further reinforced by the *PLO*. Furthermore, there are tensions between the right to a fair trial and to test out the evidence of the local authority despite the cost and delay factors, and the practice of protecting parents from being exposed to evidence which may be distressing and judgments which may have both intended and unintended consequences. Davis maintained the entire system operated to ration access to courts and to keep cases away from judicial oversight and determination. Furthermore, Davis, Cretney and Collins (1994) found the culture and ethos of achieving settlement in cases was highly 'pervasive' (Eekelaar, 2011:314). The settlement culture does not take account of the imbalance of power between the state, in the guise of the local authority, and parents. Achieving case resolution within quasi-judicial spaces is not without difficulty. Diverting cases away from court with the use of s. 20 CA89 to accommodate a child may appear consistent with the principle of partnership working under the CA89, in achieving consensual solutions, but the parents may not have the opportunity to challenge the local authority and indeed may agree to accommodation rather than face the risk of a care order being made. It is a concern that, in an attempt to either divert or resolve cases without judicial oversight, the evidence may never be properly challenged.

Decision-making: skill and judgment

In regard to difficulties of fair and inclusive decision-making in the context of child protection, commentators have argued that the *PLO*, introduced in April 2008, holds out the promise of a fairer process for parents. The overarching aim of the revised protocol is to reduce costs and delay in the management of CA89 public law cases, but in placing greater emphasis on *pre*-proceedings work, the *PLO* tasks local authorities to engage earlier and more effectively with parents (Broadhurst and Holt, 2010).

Given that the *PLO* does have the potential to increase the volume of complex child care cases that are dealt with in *quasi-judicial* settings rather than the matter being dealt with before the court, it is even more critical to interrogate the quality of both independent challenges to the local authority's plans and quality of representation for parents. Here, we are reminded of the work of Packman et al. (1986) that pre-dated the

CA89, but nevertheless raised questions about the voluntary accommodation of children in the context of child protection practice. A recent
study (Holt et al., 2013) highlighted that s. 20 CA89 accommodation
had been used in almost every case. Whilst there may be good reason for
local authorities to accommodate children under s. 20 CA89, the author
expresses concern that this may be a strategy used to further divert cases
away from court, potentially creating further delay for children who are
either on the edge of care or where the situation is too complex and the
placement is vulnerable to breakdown.

Furthermore, what any legislative instrument cannot guarantee, is
complementarity of legislative intents and institutional *practices* (Farrell,
2001). It has been argued that institutional constraints can eclipse
legislative mandate. Ongoing difficulties in English social work services
with respect to staffing levels and quality foster care – key ingredients of
effective mediated solutions, the restriction of which would, for example,
undermine appropriate support to kin – will, as Farrell suggests, mean
that the vision of the *PLO* will be eclipsed by institutional constraints.

The decision to remove a child from the care of his or her parents and
place the child in the care of local authorities is acknowledged as being
incredibly difficult – relying on professional skill and judgment (Maclean
and Kurczewski, 2011). Moreover, The *Family Justice Review* highlights
the need to have the most experienced and skilled professionals involved
in these very difficult decisions.

With the introduction of hot-desking, home-working and the increasing bureaucratization of social work, spatial separation between worker
and service is further increased creating real obstacles to effective relationship-based work (Fergusson, 2010). Spatial separation is but one
aspect of 'modernized' services; we might also postulate an affective
separation. The practice of social work assessments is now increasingly
detached from the traditional practice of home-visiting. This is an important observation as studies have consistently linked effective home-visiting as crucial in good child protection practice (Barker, 1998; Thoburn et
al., 2005; Gray, 2009). Social workers are increasingly anchored to the
computer and ICT programs in response to the demands of 'modernized' practices, a circumstance which takes away the opportunity to elicit
the rich narratives from children and their families that inform practice.

Whilst the rhetoric of achieving strong partnerships with families is
laudable, these aspirations are difficult for social workers to achieve in the
context of a profession that continues to see an increase in regulation

and bureaucracy (Broadhurst and Holt, 2010). The recommendations in the Munro review are indeed positive for the profession, but they must be viewed within a wider political context.

Therefore, the emphasis to be found in the Munro review on removing obstacles to effective practice, such as excessive bureaucracy, is welcomed, but it only addresses part of the problem. Whilst local authorities are currently introducing the recommendations of the Munro Report, they are simultaneously bracing themselves for the increased bureaucratic and practice demands introduced by the Family Justice Review. In addition, the daily interactions between practitioners operating within the family justice system need to be contextualized within a wider political landscape. In particular, it is essential that we recognize the possible implications for all practitioners and parents of the policy changes introduced by the Coalition government (Featherstone, Broadhurst and Holt, 2011).

The *PLO* (MoJ, 2008), *Family Justice Review* (MoJ, 2011a) and the *Government Response to the Family Justice Review* (MoJ and DfE, 2012) all aspire to improve partnership working whilst at the same time all three documents introduce further regulation and procedure for practitioners at a time when there are is no matching increase in resources. How can we claim to build strong multi-professional working to create a family justice service in a context of diminishing rights including the right to justice? Where levels of trust with the local authority are lower and the availability of practitioner time reduced it is even more crucial that families have access to good independent advocacy. The letter before proceedings explicitly states that parents have a right to representation. It is untimely that the government has made accessing legal help more difficult by recently introducing significant and wide-ranging changes to legal funding – resulting in families being unable to challenge or seek a review for decisions which have far-reaching consequences. This does not appear to support the building of a service that we can be proud of (Holt and Kelly, 2012b)

An effective family justice system is needed to support the making of these important decisions. It must be one that provides both children and families with an opportunity to have their own views heard in the decisions that will be made; provides proper safeguards to ensure vulnerable children and families are protected; enables and encourages out-of-court resolution, where this is appropriate; and ensures there is proportionate and skilfully managed court involvement (MoJ, 2011a).

Despite the rhetoric, there appears no relief from the procedural and managerial processes set within a context of public sector cuts affecting all professionals tasked with protecting children. Despite the skill, commitment and dedication of frontline professionals, the task of balancing the need to manage a high number of ongoing cases at the pre-proceedings stage with dealing with the additional demands when cases go to court is a challenge. There is concern that in an attempt to comply with the requirements of the *PLO* some cases will be delayed from having the oversight of the court at an earlier stage. Once in proceedings, there may be further holdups due to the necessary assessments not having been undertaken or additional assessments being sought by the parties, thus adding further delay in achieving case resolution and permanency for children (Broadhurst and Holt, 2010).

On-the-spot question	How can we ensure that children are not left holding the risk for too long to allow professionals and parents time to comply with procedures that are really aimed at reducing costs?

Further development: a way forward

Importantly, the family justice system needs to ensure there is proportionate and skilfully managed court involvement; this requires both training and management to ensure the continuing professional development of members of the judiciary (*Family Justice Review*, MoJ, 2011a). Studies have found that parents struggle to make sense of the court process; whilst attempts may be made to offer explanation to parents, processes can confuse and alienate. Appearing in court can be stressful for all parties, but as Freeman & Hunt's (1998) study highlighted, parents can experience stress even outside of the courtroom. For parents, simply waiting to enter court can be difficult on account of the lack of privacy coupled with a sense of anxiety and shame (Lindley, 1994b). Research has also found that parents can perceive their statements as inconsequential when weighted against those of professionals (Brophy, 2006). Of course, the conversion rates of local authority applications to the granting of orders by the courts, appear to bear this out (cf. Welbourne, 2008 for a fuller discussion). Parents are only too aware of the contradictions within law and practice, and that their rights as parents can be significantly curtailed where allegations of significant harm are made (Farmer and Owen, 1995). Members of the judiciary are tasked with navigating this tension and ensuring that a fair process is facilitated – at the same time as case-managing an increasing volume of the most complex work.

Notwithstanding the challenges faced by the system, professionals who work in this area are both dedicated and capable – there is a high degree of skill and stress involved in the work. In many areas there is evidence of good innovative practice and attempts to improve the way the system works. However, despite this, the system is under considerable strain with cases that should not be in proceedings, lengthy delays and rising costs (*Family Justice Review*, MoJ, 2011a).

The strain continues with increased expectations on frontline workers at the pre-proceedings stage, an increased volume of applications, and the task to conclude cases in a timely manner to avoid delay in planning for children is resulting in a system that is untenable. Representation for parents during all stages of this process has never been more crucial (Masson, 2008). The publication of the *Family Justice Review* (MoJ, 2011a), the recommendations which have been endorsed in the *Government Response* (MoJ and DfE, 2012), is perhaps a good opportunity to create a family justice service embracing the recent initiative of the College of Social Work together with the Bar Council and Law Society to further develop the aspirations of the review and to develop a training schedule for all practitioners within the service – embracing and recognizing the strengths of all professionals who work within it.

The Coalition's vision for the improvement of social work is clearly to strengthen frontline practice by reducing the bureaucratic burden on practitioners (Featherstone, Broadhurst and Holt, 2011). Moreover, we must consider the impact of sustained public sector cuts upon the ability of the local authority and, in particular, social workers to ensure justice is achieved for children and families within a protocol that necessitates resources and financing.

There appears no relief from the number of families who are seeking help from the service. There are no accurate costs but with an estimate for public law to the government alone of £0.95bn in 2009–2010, this is a system undoubtedly under strain (*Family Justice Review*, MoJ, 2011a). The number of care applications continues to rise – 20,000 in 2006 and 26,000 in 2009. In 1989 the expected length of proceedings was 12 weeks and in 2010 the average case took 53 weeks, with some cases taking considerably longer. The most recent figures show that the average care/supervision case takes 56 weeks (61 weeks within care centres) (*Family Justice Review*, MoJ, 2011a). The pressure on all professionals to deliver timely decision-making in the most complex cases both pre-proceedings and when a case is before the court is considerable.

The cumulative impact of austerity measures within the local authority and changes to legal funding will inevitably undermine effective partnership working in this area. The *Family Justice Review* highlights the importance of creating a service for the future that prioritizes the needs of children. Importantly, the review highlights the role of all professionals in achieving an effective family justice service for children and their families who turn to it at times of crisis. However, with no increase in resources to facilitate these changes the question remains as to whether the recommendations of the *Family Justice Review* will be little more than rhetoric and the reality on the ground will continue to be fragmented and reactive. There is a real opportunity to embrace the prospect of a service that firmly puts children and families at its heart, but the service needs adequate resources to ensure a fair system that we can all be proud of (Blacklaws and Lickorish Quinn, 2010).

Summary

The impetus to resolve matters without the oversight of the court is clear in a system that is creaking at the seams. There are fortunes and foibles of increased regulation and procedure – the aspirations of the *PLO* are convincing, but they cannot be effective in isolation of an understanding of and response to the wider political context (Broadhurst and Holt, 2010).

Moreover, whilst the principle of the *PLO* is laudable, there are tensions and dilemmas in relation to how the system protects families when they turn to it at times of great stress. In many ways the system appears to be mirroring the same stress and conflict without a coherent plan of how to resolve the crisis. Central to reducing the number of cases which go to court are the pre-proceedings meetings – these are formal meetings where the local authority, parents and legal representatives meet in an attempt to find consensual solutions to avoid wherever possible having to initiate court proceedings. However, we must be cautious about creating a 'settlement culture' when so much is at stake for families. Diverting cases away from court in an attempt to reduce the burden on the courts may in effect place that burden elsewhere.

Public law child care decisions are life-changing for children and their families and it is important to highlight the need for the most experienced of social work and legal professionals to be involved in this process (*Family Justice Review*, MoJ, 2011a).

There is a real challenge to look at the performance of the system as a whole – organizations are complicated and overlapping and individuals and organizations across different parts of the family justice system too often do not understand or trust each other. The report of the *Family Justice Review* highlights the tensions, but gives hope that essentially we have a strong legislative framework which prioritizes the welfare of the child and a dedicated and capable workforce who are involved in making some of the most difficult decisions, which are hugely demanding and often highly stressful (MoJ, 2011a).

On-the-spot question

Do you consider the aspirations of the *Family Justice Review* achievable in the current economic and political climate?

Further reading

Ministry of Justice (2008) *Public Law Outline* provides information on the important changes introduced with the *PLO* to divert cases, wherever safe and possible to do so, away from court.

Ministry of Justice (2011) *Family Justice Review: Final Report*. The final report of the review of the family justice system.

Ministry of Justice (2013) Practice Direction 36C: Pilot scheme: care and supervision proceedings and other proceedings under Part 4 of the Children Act 1989. This Practice Direction provides detailed directions for child care law proceedings.

Ministry of Justice and Department for Education (2012) *The Government Response to the Family Justice Review: A System with Children and Families at its Heart*. The government response to a comprehensive review of the family justice system.

6

PREPARING TO GO TO COURT

The importance of recording

> Not everything that can be counted counts, and not everything that counts can be counted.
>
> *Munro, 2011:45*

As Munro suggests above, there will always be accountability in social work practice and there is no doubt that recording provides evidence to the organization that practitioners have complied with organizational goals and expectations. Furthermore, keeping a record of involvement with the family will provide evidence in other contexts – for example, conferences, reviews, pre-proceedings protocols and court – of the nature and level of contact that has taken place, giving important details and analysis of any involvement. Whilst the organizational culture may require *boxes to be ticked*, a *cut-and-paste* culture is not helpful when using recording as the basis of an assessment.

According to Munro: 'Complying with prescription and keeping records to demonstrate compliance has become too dominant.' (2011:8) It is important that social workers provide a critical, analytical and reflective account of the work undertaken with families. This level of analysis requires experience, skill and a sound professional judgment grounded in theory and research.

> Whether to record a decision is a risk decision in itself which should, to a large extent, be left to professional judgment. The decision whether or not to make a record, however, and the extent of that record, should be made after considering the likelihood of harm occurring and its seriousness.
>
> *Munro, 2011:4*

These decisions highlight the need for social workers to be skilled and experienced. It is imperative that standards for entry into the profession remain high – social work practitioners are required to have excellent communication skills. Recording information is a skill that requires a high standard of detail together with an ability to provide an overview and analysis of the information. This was a theme echoed in the review of child deaths (Munro, 1996) where more than half of the reviews examined fell below an acceptable standard of recording because specific details of contacts were missing, coupled with factual inaccuracies and a lack of coherence. Furthermore, Dorota Iwaniec et al. (2004) highlighted the presence of lots of information but found that a general lack of coherence, analysis and overview was evident in recordings.

Records are pivotal in providing information to support a good assessment. Records inform decision-making, planning and review. Crucially, record-keeping provides evidence in formal settings. The knowledge that your records could be requested either by the court, or in a request under the Data Protection Act 1998, and that you may need to defend your records should serve as a reminder of the importance of accurate recording.

| *On-the-spot question* | How do you ensure you record information to comply with these requirements? |

Fact/opinion

Factual information informs the court of what happened – it provides the facts in the case from the people who are directly involved in the events. Documents, objects, video-recording etc. can also form part of the facts of the case. The key is to ensure proximity to the events – direct involvement as opposed to obtaining details from third parties which is considered by the court as hearsay evidence and, although admissible in care proceedings, it will be less persuasive than direct contact with the events outlined. This is important to remember when so much information is *gathered* from other sources and *shoe-horned* into the assessment document. It is imperative that recordings are clear about what information has been obtained *first-hand* and what has been *gathered* in the process of undertaking an assessment. Including information from other professionals is inevitable, but if the balance of information is obtained in this manner, the court will need to be satisfied the information has been verified and corroborated by the author. The reliance upon third-party information to form an assessment will inevitably remove the practitioner from ownership of the detail and this is potentially problematic as it will impact on the competence and confidence to express an opinion on the facts and to take risks. It is a significant correlation that an increase in risk-averse practices has developed alongside a reliance on electronic data systems where the organizational agenda for gathering information is prioritized over the need for a critical, analytical and evaluative assessment based on detailed knowledge of the family which has evolved over a period of time.

Professionals must be able to provide an opinion based on expertise *Re R (A Minor) (Expert Evidence)* [1991] – this requires skill, experience and confidence (Holt et al., 2013). Expertise can be established by formal qualifications, length of experience and by demonstrating a detailed knowledge of the relevant area of practice. It is unhelpful both to the family and the court to produce a list of facts/data without an expert opinion on what judgment is made on the information, and what action and by whom is required to reduce risk and the consequences if the risk is not reduced. It is important to consider that what you write will be a permanent record for the family and will be read by them, other professionals and may be used as evidence in court proceedings. It is also important to remember some key rules when recording information. I always advise practitioners that they may be cross-examined on their written records therefore it is important to ensure that you can defend what you have recorded.

Information should be recorded in a just and fair manner to ensure justice is achieved for the family. Information recorded must be accurate and an analysis of the facts should produce a reasonable and proportionate response to the presenting issue, reflecting a good level of communication and consultation with the family during the process of the assessment.

Use of language

Reports and recordings have the potential to be circulated to other parties prior to the author of these documents having the opportunity to be heard. The information contained within documents will set the tone for any subsequent interaction and is therefore pivotal in the process.

Language needs to be clear and unambiguous, but also balanced and respectful to the family and other professionals. It is often too easy to identify from records when practitioners were personally affected by events and recording can reflect anger/frustration with emphasis being placed on emotive words. It is important to retain a balanced, proportionate response that is reasonable, rather than provide an emotional response, which is arguably more difficult to defend.

Avoid the use of clichés – they are not particularly helpful and could be applied to any number of situations. Referring to a family as being *on a journey* provides no useful additional information and is likely to attract a line of questioning that is to be avoided. There are many stylistic hazards, as outlined by Hopkins (1998), which include repetition, over-stating the obvious, padding, empty phrases and clichés. Information recorded must have a purpose and the principles contained in the Data Protection Act 1998 necessitate that records should be *adequate, relevant* and *not excessive.*

Preparation of reports

Report-writing is a skill requiring, as a minimum, a high standard of liter-acy. A good report is dependent on accurate and detailed recordings that are tailored to the specific child/family. Information should be clear, with a logical argument, including analysis of the information leading to a clear conclusion. Facts and opinions must be made clear within the report. It is deeply concerning when, due to work pressures, reports are *cut and pasted* from other documents in an attempt to save time. This problem was highlighted when a mother stated to the social worker in a child protection conference: 'the report is very good, but it is one you prepared earlier. These are not my kids – I have three, not five. I don't suppose you know who has got my kids.' It was clear the social worker had migrated information from one document to another to save time, but the impression given to the parent and other professionals is poor.

Statements

The primary purpose of a statement is to set out the factual evidence of the case so that everyone knows in advance exactly the evidence which is being presented to the court. A good statement provides clarity in the proceedings and this has to be in the interest of all parties. A badly writ-ten statement can lead to misunderstandings, prolonged litigation and hours of cross-examination. So time spent on the preparation of state-ments is invaluable.

Whilst there is no formally defined format to writing a statement, the Practice Direction: Protocol for judicial case management in public law Children Act cases sets out the requirements for the initial social work statement as follows:

The initial social work statement filed by the LA [local authority] within 2 days of the issue of an application is strictly limited to the following evidence:

- The precipitating incident(s) and background circumstances relevant to the grounds and reasons for making the application including a brief description of any referral and assessment processes that have already occurred
- Any facts and matters that are within the social worker's personal knowledge
- Any emergency steps and previous court orders that are relevant to the application
- Any decisions made by the LA that are relevant to the application
- Information relevant to the ethnicity, language, religion, culture, gender and vulnerability of the child and other significant persons in the form of a 'family profile' together with a narrative description and details of the social care services that are relevant to the same
- Where the LA is applying for an ICO [interim care order] and/or is proposing to remove or seeking to continue the removal of a child under emergency protection, the LA's initial proposals for the child, including placement, contact with parents and other significant persons and the social care services that are proposed
- The LA's initial proposals for the further assessment of the parties during the proceedings including twin track planning
- The social work timetable, tasks and responsibilities so far as they are known.

Appendix B3

The revised *PLO* introduced in 2013 requires the local authority to provide a focused and succinct summary of important dates and events in the child's life with an emphasis on assessment and analysis, as opposed to enormously voluminous materials that are largely historical and descriptive (Practice Direction 36C: this Practice Direction supplements FPR Part 36, r. 36.2 (Transitional arrangements and pilot schemes)).

Giving evidence in court

Giving evidence in court provokes anxiety amongst even the most experienced practitioners. However, the advice I give to practitioners is that having a detailed knowledge and understanding of the child and family, together with evidence that is proportionate, reasonable and fair, will be difficult to dispute. Conversely, a scant knowledge of the family, together with an approach that is both inflexible and resistant to the consideration of alternatives, has the potential to attract lengthy cross-examination. It is incredibly difficult to challenge a witness with expert knowledge and understanding who is fair, proportionate and reasonable. It is imperative that social workers understand and have complied with any legal requirements and relevant guidance and have considered the range of options available to the court in their assessment.

It is important when preparing statements and reports for court to remember that these documents need to contain the full facts and case notes may be requested by the court if evidence is not agreed or there is a dispute over the facts. Preparation for court is essential – reading over notes/statements/reports is strongly advised to ensure clarity of information and to anticipate obvious questions which may be asked if evidence is required. Furthermore, attempt to pre-empt areas where you are likely to be challenged and be clear about your decision-making and reasons for taking any resulting action, considering any alternative actions and reasons for not pursuing these.

Whilst there is no stipulated dress code, you need to show respect to the court in terms of your behaviour and dress to reflect a professional approach appropriate for the occasion.

If you are required to give evidence in court you will be invited to either stand or sit in the witness box. It is a matter for you as to which you prefer, but my advice is, wherever practicable, it is better to stand as you will be more visible and your evidence needs to be heard clearly by the court. Whether sitting or standing in the witness box, face the lower half of your body towards the justices or judge at all times, turning the upper half of your body to receive questions and turning back towards the justices or judge to give answers. This is important as it is the justices or judges who need to hear your evidence and it will avoid any repeat questions being asked by advocates before you have the opportunity to give your response to the question asked.

Give only direct evidence, that is your own first-hand evidence, as far as possible, making sure that the source of any second-hand (hearsay) evidence is identified. Ensure any opinions given are grounded in facts and justified by your experience and professional qualifications.

If you do not know the answer it is important to state that, rather than attempting to conceal your lack of knowledge. In the event of you not being able to either hear the question being asked or you do not understand the question, it is important that you ask for the question to be repeated or explained further. The court is relying on your evidence, so it is fundamental that you are clear about what is being asked of you.

Use of experts

Detailed guidance on the use of experts can be found in the Practice Direction 25A: Experts and assessors in family proceedings 2010. The general rule in family proceedings is that the court's permission is required to call an expert or to put in evidence an expert's report r. 25.4(1). In addition, in proceedings that relate to children, the court's permission is required to instruct an expert r. 12.74(1).

An expert witness's main function is to provide an independent expert opinion to the court based on the information provided by those instructing the expert. An expert in family proceedings has an overriding duty to the court that takes precedence over any obligation to the person from whom the expert has received instructions or by whom the expert is paid (para. 3.1 Practice Direction 25A).

Proceedings in respect of children are confidential and, without the permission of the court, disclosure of information and documents relating to proceedings may amount to a contempt of court as confidentiality must be protected. The sharing of any information with an expert must only be undertaken when permission of the court has been obtained under r. 12.73 and r. 14.14. Furthermore, the court's permission is needed if a child subject to proceedings is required to have an examination for the purpose of preparing expert evidence to be used as part of the proceedings (r. 12.20).

Before permission is obtained from the court to instruct an expert in proceedings relating to a child, it will be necessary for the party seeking permission to make enquiries of the expert in order to provide the court with information to enable it to decide whether to give permission. In practice, enquiries may need to be made of more than one expert for this purpose.

The increase in the number of care applications has been reflected in an increased use of experts. Whilst it may be entirely appropriate to obtain an expert opinion on a complex medical issue, for example, the routine instruction of multiple experts, including independent social work assessments, is now being questioned (MoJ, 2011a). Whilst obtaining an independent assessment in a small number of cases may be reasonable and fair, routinely commissioning assessments whilst social workers are left case-managing is problematic for a number of reasons. Firstly, it removes the social worker from regular contact with the child and family, often reducing contact to just formal meetings. Secondly, it builds in additional delay for the child who is left waiting whilst instructed experts report back to the court. Finally, the cost implications of routinely instructing experts have been recently reviewed in the modernization agenda of the family court. The train is set for a reduction in the time for a care application to be concluded to 26 weeks, which will inevitably result in a reduction in the use of experts in proceedings and the local authority will be expected to have completed all specialist assessments pre-proceedings, unless the situation is an emergency (Holt et al., 2013).

> **KEY CASE ANALYSIS**

Re Avon, North Somerset and Gloucestershire Public Law Case No 1 [2013]

The facts of this case are that the local authority applied for care and placement orders in respect of two children. The parents conceded that they could not care for the children but the maternal grandmother applied for a special guardianship order in respect of one child (accepting that she could not care for both children). The Local Authority withdrew its opposition to one child remaining in the care of the grandmother on the third day of the final hearing.

In his judgment HHJ Wildblood QC stated the following: 'There had been too many expert reports, it had not been "necessary" in the new language of Part 25 (or indeed reasonably required) for there to be reports from a psychologist, an independent social worker, a specialist guardianship social worker, a local authority social worker and a guardian.'

The case had taken 58 weeks to final hearing in circumstances that HHJ Wildblood stated 'ought not to have been necessary'.

Children in court

Until fairly recently the presumption in family law proceedings was that it was undesirable for a child to be required to give oral evidence as part of the proceedings and doing so was an extremely rare event.

> **KEY CASE ANALYSIS**

Re W (Children) (Abuse: Oral Evidence) [2010]

The Supreme Court in *Re W (Children) (Abuse: Oral Evidence)* [2010] reviewed this presumption prompting a sea-change in the law in this area. The presumption against a child giving evidence in family proceedings could not be reconciled with the jurisprudence of the ECtHR which required a fair balance to be struck between the competing ECHR rights of those involved, in particular Articles 6 and 8.

The Supreme Court has ruled that children can be brought in as witnesses in family law cases, providing the benefits of doing so outweigh the risk of harm to the child. The court indicated that sufficient justification would be needed before a child was called to give evidence. The essence of the court's decision is whether justice can be done to all parties if the child is not allowed to be heard in evidence.

In determining if a child should be allowed to give evidence in proceedings the court must give consideration to a two-stage test and weigh up: (a) the advantages the oral evidence will bring to the determination of the truth; and (b) the damage or harm that giving evidence may do to the child in question or any other child.

Among the areas that must be considered are a child's age and maturity, the child's own wishes and feelings about giving evidence and the wishes and feelings of the child's parents or other persons with parental responsibility. Any child who is unwilling to attend court should not be forced to do so.

This is a relatively recent development in case law and, as such, only time will tell as to how family judges interpret and apply the principles set down by the Supreme Court with regards child witnesses. The principles will undoubtedly be considered and applied on the merits of each individual case, and, as with all aspects of the law relating to children, the welfare of the child is paramount. The court will not sanction a child giving evidence in proceedings where this would pose a risk of harm.

The role of Cafcass

The guardian ad litem (GAL) service was first identified in England in 1973 following the death of Maria Colwell. Maria had been the subject of a care order and was living in foster care with relatives. Maria's mother applied for the order to be revoked stating that she wished Maria to be returned to her care. The local authority did not oppose the application for revocation of the order and Maria was subsequently returned to the care of her mother. Maria tragically died in her parents' care and there was a Committee of Inquiry appointed to consider lessons to be learned. The Committee of Inquiry concluded:

> ... had the views of an independent social worker been available to the court it would have had the assistance of a second opinion which might or might not have endorsed the conclusions and recommendations contained in ... [the social work] report.
>
> *Committee of Inquiry into the Care and Supervision Provided in*
> *Relation to Maria Colwell, 1974*

The tragic events surrounding Maria's death prompted significant changes to the procedures for protecting children at risk of abuse. The role of the GAL was extended in England and Wales to include children who are the subject of adoption and a range of care and related proceedings. This role was further reinforced with the CA89 making it possible to appoint a GAL in all specified proceedings and retaining the role of the GAL in adoption proceedings.

Cafcass was established on 1 April 2001 as an independent organization which unified the family court services previously provided by the Family Court Welfare Service, the Guardian ad Litem Service and the Children's Division of the Official Solicitor's Office. The GAL was replaced by the term 'family court advisor' (FCA).

The role of Cafcass is to safeguard and promote the welfare of children; give advice to the family courts; make provision for children to be represented; and provide information, advice and support to children and their families. The principle role of the FCA is to advise the court on what he or she considers to be in the best interests of the child. The role of the FCA involves drawing to the court's attention all relevant matters to assist in a finding-of-fact exercise (see *Re Lancashire County Council v D and E* [2008] para. 19).

An FCA may be appointed when the local authority makes an application for a care or supervision order, or, alternatively, in private law applications when parents who are separating or divorcing cannot agree arrangements in respect of their child.

> ◤ **PRACTICE FOCUS**
>
> Referring back to the case study of Jasper and Nancy (see page 13), an FCA has been appointed for Jasper and upon reading the papers is satisfied that the local authority is acting appropriately to ensure Jasper's welfare is protected. The FCA requests leave from the court to withdraw from the proceedings as she is in agreement with the care plan for Jasper and can therefore see no further role for Cafcass. The court refuses this request on the basis that continued involvement is required due to the complexity of Nancy's needs and the requirement for Jasper's needs to be to independently represented in the proceeedings so the court does not lose sight of this given Nancy's complex health needs which have continued to predominate the proceedings thus far.
>
> Do you agree with the judge in this case?

The FCA is appointed to represent the views of the child in court and to ensure that the child's wishes and feelings are known to the court. The FCA, therefore, has a pivotal role in ensuring the welfare of the child and that the court timetable is child-focused avoiding unnecessary delay for the child. FCAs are qualified social workers with substantial experience of child care matters and a comprehensive understanding of family law. The FCA will need to be an experienced, confident, competent practitioner with excellent interpersonal skills and a sharp analytical approach to complex issues involving families who are often hard to reach, and with the ability to deal with a range of professionals with whom there may be differences of professional opinion and complex evidence to navigate. The FCA is appointed to provide an independent opinion to the court. In order to achieve this aim the FCA will make an assessment based on interviews and visits to all parties involved in the case. The FCA will produce a report and make recommendations to the court. All parties with leave of the court will have an opportunity to see the report before the final hearing (r. 4.23/r.23 (Family Proceedings Courts (Children Act 1989) Rules 1991 and FPR 1991)).

The child's solicitor is responsible for presenting the child's case in court. In some circumstances the child may not agree with the assessment, recommendation or both of the FCA. If the child is of an age and level of understanding where he/she is able to express a view, the solicitor must then act for the child and advise the court when this is in conflict with the opinion of the FCA (*Re S (Independent Representation)* [1993]).

The court will allow children to participate in proceedings if they are considered to be of sufficient age, intelligence, maturity and understanding. Moreover, a child may make an application to remove the FCA, so as to enable the child to participate directly in the proceedings (Family Proceedings Rules 1991, r. 9.2A(4)).

Furthermore, there is an important role for Cafcass when cases are not before the court. An amendment to s. 26 CA89 (made by the Adoption and Children Act 2002) created a statutory duty to appoint an IRO to participate in case reviews, monitor the local authority's performance in reviews and consider whether it would be appropriate to refer cases to Cafcass. The Children and Family Court Advisory and Support Service (Reviewed Case Referral) Regulations 2004, made under s. 26 CA89, extend the functions of Cafcass so that, on a referral from an IRO, Cafcass can consider bringing proceedings for breaches of the child's human rights, judicial review and other proceedings. It means that a guardian can be appointed in a case that is not before the court and may not involve a child who is subject to an order or proceedings and it is a role imposed on Cafcass not by the court but by an individual IRO.

The report, *The Work of the Independent Reviewing Officer* (Cafcass, 2006), a survey of local authorities about the application of s. 118 Adoption and Children Act 2002, identified that no child had ever been referred to Cafcass by any IRO.

The Coventry and Warwickshire Pre-Proceedings Pilot with a third pilot site (Liverpool) is ongoing. The pilot project, which commenced in January 2011, introduced the FCA into pre-proceedings social work to examine whether earlier involvement and the expertise of the FCA could impact positively on pre-proceedings social work and contribute to a reduction in delay in care proceedings within the court area. The pilot project's designers considered that earlier involvement might support:

- safe and effective diversion of 'edge of care' cases wherever possible;
- improved pre-proceedings social work assessment and decision-making such that duration of care proceedings was reduced.

The pilot aimed to narrow the issues brought before the courts should care proceedings be issued and equally provide the FCA with a 'head start' given the importance of an early, effective steer from the FCA to case management in care proceedings. Given the absence of an independent voice for the child within pre-proceedings, the FCA would also provide a critical role in ensuring that the welfare of the child remained central to decision-making (Broadhurst and Holt, 2012).

The impact of public sector cuts and rising care demand over the duration of the project is noted. Resources are stretched to impossible limits in respect of all agencies and this impacts on court sitting time, FCA continuity, social work continuity, the timely filing of statements, the input that private practice lawyers can provide to parents and timely response to local authority evidence. That demand exceeds supply is without doubt a clear concern amongst all agencies with local practitioners describing an acutely difficult climate in the context of unprecedented public sector cuts. The Liverpool project has also taken a 'whole system' approach to change, based on an understanding that, despite best intentions, any attempt to invoke change in complex systems will likely be unsuccessful where intervention fails to approach system change holistically. Whilst putting the FCA in all pre-proceedings cases is probably not feasible, there may be an important additional role for the FCA within the pre-proceedings stage, perhaps at an earlier point to stimulate good pre-proceedings practice (Broadhurst et al., 2013).

Professional advocacy for families

The work of the London-based FRG has done much to delineate how good practice in regard to independent professional advocacy for families involved with child protection services might be organized (Featherstone, Fraser, Ashley and Ledward, 2011). In a detailed evaluative study, the impact of professional advocacy was clear: 97 per cent of parents and family members felt the advocacy service had been helpful and 46 per cent felt it had made a difference to the outcome of their case (Featherstone, Fraser et al., 2011). Evaluative findings indicate what can be done, when advocacy is done *well.* The following extract from the Code for Professional Advocates (2009) drawn up by the FRG is pertinent:

> Advocacy means assisting people to make informed choices, not making decisions for them. The advocate's role is to enable the service user to have their voice heard, to participate, as far as practicable, in the decisions being made about their child and to have their viewpoint taken into account, whilst avoiding any action which may or may be seen to collude with potentially placing a child at risk of harm.
>
> *FRG, 2009:3*

Summary

The government makes a commitment to better training for social workers in court preparation and presentation skills. What it does not promise is more resources to address the problem of overstretched social workers whose workloads are already too high and who are ill-equipped to meet the demands they currently face, let alone raise their game to undertake 'more high quality work with children and families' in order to 'ensure more credible evidence is put before the Courts' (MoJ and DfE, 2012:14, para. 47). The proposed statutory guillotine on completing care cases is simply a distraction from the need for resources to be channelled to address the causes of delay (Gore, 2012).

The reality of these cases is that many months are lost in court proceedings due to a lack of court time, inefficiency and poor planning at the outset of proceedings – the failure of local authorities to set up assessments in parallel with initiating proceedings or dealing with immediate and pressing issues of placement, and due to a lack of local authority in-house resources building in further delay to assessments. The government has recognized that:

> The quality and timeliness of social care assessments put to the courts has a crucial bearing on how quickly cases progress. Poor or late assessments can lead to delayed or re-scheduled hearings and can result in courts commissioning evidence-gathering elsewhere.
>
> *MoJ and DfE, 2012:14, para. 45*

On-the-spot question   How do we ensure children remain central in all assessments and plans, and yet achieve timely decision-making?

There is no doubt that greater emphasis will be placed on achieving consensual solutions outside of the court. Whilst this is good practice, it requires a whole-system approach and to be appropriately resourced (Broadhurst et al., 2013; Masson et al., 2013).

Further reading

Davis, L (2007) *See You in Court: A Social Worker's Guide to Presenting Evidence in Care Proceedings.* This book provides a practical guide for social workers who are preparing to go to court.

Family Rights Group (2009) *Professional Advocacy Services, Principles and Standards.* This provides guidance on the standards provided by the FRG for professional advocacy services.

Featherstone, B and C Fraser (2012) '"I'm just a mother, I'm nothing special, they're all professionals": parental advocacy as an aid to parental engagement' 17(2) *Child and Family Social Work* 244–53. This paper highlights the importance of providing advocacy to parents to aid parental engagement.

7
CONCLUDING COMMENTS

Achieving revolutionary change within a climate of austerity

There is no doubt that the direction of travel set in train by the *Family Justice Review* and the Children and Families Bill is not readily reversible (Broadhurst et al., 2013). This shifts the burden of parenting assessment to the administrative space of pre-court social work (Holt et al., 2013). Increasingly, flexibility is being introduced within the formal pre-proceedings stage where parents have been put on notice of the local authority's intention to issue care proceedings. The pre-proceedings stage may be the most appropriate location to build in flexibility, but this is not without consequences as it may result in delay being introduced at an earlier stage without judicial oversight and scrutiny (Holt et al., 2013).

The impact of austerity measures in the context of the now hege-monic concern with the timetable for the child have further contributed to a strained relationship between the local authority and parents (Featherstone, Morris and White, 2013). Achieving timely decision-making for children is, of course, important and legitimate and we have seen the consequences of delay and poor planning in respect of outcomes for children, but the concern is when the timetable for the child is used to support a modernization agenda which is principally aimed at reducing costs when a case goes to court, which indeed supports timely decision-making, but lacks the flexibility to respond to less instrumental approaches (Holt and Kelly, 2012b).

There is a revolutionary culture of change within the child protection system which has been ushered in to achieve an inquisitorial rather than an adversarial system for family justice with the path towards a single family court in 2014. In order to achieve a system that we can be proud of, we need a sustainable model of child protection that protects children and adds value to family life.

Whilst some delay in planning for children is inevitable, the *system* and *practices* have compounded problems with timely decision-making for children. The practice of seeking multi-layered expert evidence in care cases is one example of building in delay. Expert opinion is impor-tant and necessary, but we need to use the expert knowledge already located within agencies which are part of the LSCB, and in most instances these should form the overall assessment. There has been a tendency in recent years to routinely instruct independent social work assessments – this has resulted in social workers having minimal contact with families, leaving the important assessment of the family to social workers commissioned to provide reports within proceedings. Whilst in exceptional cases an independent social work assessment may be necessary, the independence of the report should be judged not on the authorship of the report, but on the quality of the assessment. In an ongoing study it is clear that, when social workers are completing detailed parenting assessments prior to court, the skill, competency and confidence of the practitioner is clearly evident and there is little or no challenge (Holt et al., 2013).

Further recent pilots, such as the tri-borough project (Beckett et al., 2013) and the Liverpool protocol (Holt et al., 2013), demonstrate that obtaining good quality assessment and management of pre-proceedings work with families significantly reduces the need to re-examine evidence in court ensuring delay is reduced at this stage.

Whilst the direction of travel introduced and supported by the *Family Justice Review* has been broadly welcomed (including by the Office of the Children's Commissioner, 2013), there is a substantive body of evidence that has identified the negative impact of delay for children who wait in interim placements where judicial case management is indecisive (MoJ, 2011a). The impact of these changes will have both intended and unintended consequences for all practitioners operating within this system to achieve case resolution swiftly with little margin for discretion and professional judgment (Broadhurst et al., 2013).

Furthermore, as family justice reforms move to reduce the length of care proceedings (MoJ, 2012), the pre-proceedings meeting will be essential because parents will have less time to retrieve their position within the court arena (Holt et al., 2013). Proposed legislative changes in the Children and Families Bill indicate a clear shift away from re-assessment of parents during court proceedings with the aim of reducing delay in the family court, emphasizing a hegemonic concern with the timetable for the child coupled with a less tolerant approach to welfare and waiting for parents to change (Grover, 2008). In this context, effective assessment, support and planning for children and their parents within pre-proceedings will be critical to facilitate engagement with local authority concerns and to maximize opportunities for rehabilitation where appropriate and safe to do so, or to make the decision to make an application to court (Holt et al., 2013).

Re Devon County Council v EB AND Others (Minors) [2013]

This was a fact-finding hearing in High Court care proceedings. The evidence involved multiple injuries on twins with a complex family medical history, resulting in the local authority being unable to prove the injuries were non-accidental to the standard required and seeking expert opinion. In his judgment Baker J emphasized the need for the court 'to survey a wider canvas' than that of the medical information in isolation and stressed that: 'in cases of suspected physical abuse the court must follow the evidence and pursue the enquiry in whatever detail and for however long is necessary to arrive at the truth'.

Baker J observed that in cases of suspected child abuse it is important that: 'There is a full and thorough forensic examination; this requires judicial continuity before a judge of sufficient experience. That, although judges will be rigorous to resist the unnecessary use of experts, equally, they will not hesitate to endorse expert instruction, under the new rules, where they are satisfied this is necessary to determine the relevant issues. That with regard to concluding cases within 26 weeks, whilst this may be possible for the vast majority, there will still be a minority of exceptional cases where investigation takes longer. Judges should be vigilant to identify these as soon as possible.'

In his judgment in the *Devon* case, Baker J is clearly highlighting the complexity of child protection cases, and how complex families don't necessarily fit into the neat linear world of prescribed timescales and procedures. A different approach was taken in *Re Avon, North Somerset and Gloucestershire Public Law Case* [2013] when HHJ Wildblood QC in judgment stated that the case had taken 58 weeks to final hearing in circumstances where that level of delay ought not to have been necessary. It is clear from recent judgments that case duration is under scrutiny, which presents a challenge for all who operate within the family justice system.

Effective child protection practice, with complex families, that place the child at the heart of the system requires a whole-system approach and a flexible workforce at all stages of the process. Diverting cases away from court and concluding cases within a prescribed time is only effective if these cases are concluded justly.

It is clear from the final report of Professor Munro (2011) that social work needs to rediscover its commitment to, and tolerance of, a relationship-based approach to working with families. A revolutionary culture of change within the family justice system, which is placing more emphasis on pre-proceedings practice, may be important in stimulating this change. Importantly, within a child protection system the child must remain central in all assessments and plans. The challenge is that, within a configured children's social care service that is largely specialized, decision-making in child protection can become lost between the remit of a safeguarding team and a court team. There is a need to review the culture of social work to ensure, for example, that a child protection plan includes the pre-proceedings protocol, and that we avoid procedures running consecutively according to the remit of the team responsible for the family, rather than procedures running concurrently, which presents a challenge when the remit of a team is highly prescriptive. Our procedures and practice must reflect the philosophy of a holistic approach to supporting children and their families reinforced in *Working Together* (DoE, 2013) and the proposals for legislative change contained within the Children and Families Bill.

Further reading

Featherstone, B, K Broadhurst and K E Holt (2011) 'Thinking systemically, thinking politically: building strong partnerships with families in the context of rising inequality?' *British Journal of Social Work*. The paper provides a review of the literature and research evidence that examines the current tensions of achieving partnership working within the context of austerity and inequality.

Masson, J M, J Dickens, K F Bader and J Young (2013) *Partnership by Law? The Pre-proceedings Process for Families on the Edge of Care Proceedings*. A study that examines the pre-proceedings process for families on the edge of care.

Munby, Sir James (2013) 'View From The President's Chambers (6): The process of reform – latest developments'. This article provides an update from the President of the Family Division on the implementation of the revised *PLO* and plans for a single family court in 2014.

USEFUL WEBSITES

Association of Lawyers for Children
www.alc.org.uk

Cafcass
www.cafcass.gov.uk

Department for Education: The Children and Families Bill 2013
www.education.gov.uk/a00221161/

Department for Education: Local Safeguarding Children Boards
www.education.gov.uk/childrenandyoungpeople/safeguardingchildren/
protection/b002 9380/lscb

Department for Education: *Working Together*
www.education.gov.uk/aboutdfe/statutory/g00213160/working-together-
to-safeguard-children

Family Justice Council
www.judiciary.gov.uk/about-the-judiciary/advisory-bodies/fjc

Family Rights Group
www.frg.org.uk

Nagalro
www.nagalro.com

UNICEF UK: The United Nations Children's Fund
www.unicef.org.uk/crc?gclid=CID40OeY6boCFbLJtAodSwsAoQ&sissr=1

Voice Advocacy
www.voiceyp.org/professionalzone/advocacy?gclid=ClbAiN6c6boCFfHKtAod
GQcAXQ

GLOSSARY

Assessment

A good social work assessment requires deep analysis and critical reflection of the developmental needs of the child (being able to address all the questions in the CA89 s. 1 welfare checklist) and importantly the level of risk the child is or is likely to be exposed to. Furthermore, the strengths of each individual within the family and the family collectively need to be highlighted. An assessment needs to comply with the rules of natural justice – to be reasonable, proportionate, justifiable and achieved with full consultation and participation from the child and family. An assessment is not an event, rather a process that is reviewed regularly and updated in response to changes and developments. The assessment should be sufficiently detailed to inform the decision as to whether a child is in need or is suffering or likely to suffer significant harm as defined in s. 31 CA89.

Care order

Where a local authority decides to make an application for a care order or a supervision order:

31

(2) a court may only make a care order or supervision order if it is satisfied—

    (a) that the child concerned is suffering, or is likely to suffer, significant harm; and

    (b) that the harm, or likelihood of harm, is attributable to

        (i) the care given to the child, or likely to be given to him if the order were not made, not being what it would be reasonable to expect a parent to give to him; or

        (ii) the child's being beyond parental control.

CA89

A care order is made until the child reaches 18 unless the court following an application by either the local authority or the parent discharges the order, or if the court makes a residence order or adoption order which automatically discharges the care order.

Child protection

The responsibility to care for and protect children and young people in the UK is the primary responsibility of their parents. However, where there are concerns about a child's safety or development as a result of abuse or neglect, there is provision in the CA89 for the state to intervene to protect children and young people who have suffered or likely to suffer significant harm.

Children in need

It shall be the general duty of every local authority to (a) safeguard and promote the welfare of children within their area who are in need; and (b) so far as is consistent with that duty, to promote the upbringing of such children by their families, by providing a range and level of services appropriate to those children's needs (s. 17(1) CA89). The duty applies only to children who are defined as in need (s. 17 (10) CA89).

Contact

Contact is an important aspect of the care plan and the court must consider contact arrangements as part of the care plan before the making of a care order (s. 34(11) CA89). Contact is an important aspect of the care plan for any child who is accommodated by the local authority. Where the local authority makes an application to court for a care order the court must consider contact arrangements as part of the care plan before the making of a care order (s. 34(11) CA89).

Delay

'*In any proceedings in which any question with respect to the upbringing of a child arises, the court shall have regard to the general principle that any delay in determining the question is likely to prejudice the welfare of the child.*' (s. 1(2) CA89)

Duty to investigate

The Children Act charges local authorities with the '*duty to investigate ... if they have reasonable cause to suspect that a child who lives, or is found, in their area is suffering, or is likely to suffer, significant harm*' (s. 47 CA89).

Emergency applications

If it is urgent and of necessity to either keep or remove a child to a place of safety, a local authority should wherever possible – and unless a child's safety is otherwise at immediate risk – apply for an EPO. *Working Together* says police powers to remove a child in an emergency should be used only in exceptional circumstances where there is insufficient time to seek an EPO or for reasons relating to the immediate safety of the child (*Working Together*, 2013:64).

Family court advisor

The Guardian ad Litem Service was first identified in England in 1973 following the death of a child, Maria Colwell. Cafcass was established on 1 April 2001 as an independent organization which unified the family court services previously provided by the Family Court Welfare Service, the Guardian ad Litem Service and the Children's Division of the Official Solicitor's Office. The term 'guardian ad litem' was replaced by the term 'family court advisor'.

Harm

In s. 31(9) CA89, harm is defined as '*ill-treatment or the impairment of health or development*'.

Human rights

The Human Rights Act 1998 incorporates the ECHR into UK law. The Act makes it unlawful for public authorities to act in a manner that is incompatible with the rights and freedoms contained in the Act.

Local Safeguarding Children Boards

Safeguarding and promoting the welfare of children requires effective co-ordination in every local area. Section 13 of the CA04 requires each local authority to establish an LSCB for its area and specifies the organizations and individuals (other than the local authority) that should be represented on LSCBs (*Working Together*, DfE, 2013:58). LSCBs coordinate the work to safeguard children locally and monitor and challenge the effectiveness of local arrangements. Ultimately, effective safeguarding of children can only be achieved by putting children at the centre of the system, and by every individual and agency playing its full part, working together to meet the needs of our most vulnerable children (DfE, 2013:8).

No order principle

Where a court is considering whether or not to make one or more orders under the Act with respect to a child, it shall not make the order or any of the orders unless it considers that doing so would be better for the child than making no order at all (s. 1(5) CA89).

Parental responsibility

'[A]*ll the rights, duties, powers, responsibilities and authority which by law a parent of a child has in relation to the child and his property*' (s. 3(1) CA89).

Partnership
'It is a collage of rights, duties and recommendations, only some of which are grounded in practice. A great deal of use is made of terms such as "co-operation" and "consultation", terms that are vague and that leave considerable room for interpretation and that can mean different things in different situations.' (Kaganas, 1995:4)

Public Law Outline
This Practice Direction has the overriding objective of enabling the court to deal with cases justly, having regard to the welfare issues involved. Revisions to the *Public Law Outline* included in the Practice Direction 36C: Pilot scheme: care and supervision proceedings and other proceedings under Part 4 of the Children Act 1989 support the overriding objective to ensure proportionate use of resources within the timeframe for the child.

Serious case reviews
Regulation 5 of the Local Safeguarding Children Boards Regulations 2006 requires LSCBs to undertake reviews of serious cases in the following circumstances: firstly, where a child sustains a potentially life-threatening injury or serious and permanent impairment of health and development through abuse or neglect; secondly, where a child has been seriously harmed as a result of being subject to sexual abuse; thirdly, where a parent has been murdered and a domestic homicide review is being initiated; fourthly, where a child has been seriously harmed following a violent assault perpetrated by another child or an adult, and the case gives rise to concerns about the way in which local professionals and services worked together to safeguard and promote the welfare of children. This includes inter-agency and/or interdisciplinary working

Significant harm
Significant is not defined in the CA89, although it does say that the court should compare the health and development of the child 'with that which could be reasonably expected of a similar child'. So the courts have to decide for themselves what constitutes significant harm by looking at the facts of each individual case.

Statutory review
Looked after children, regardless of their route into accommodation provided by the local authority, are required to have regular reviews. Once a care order is made, the responsibility for the child lies with the local authority, which must take responsibility as part of its corporate parenting role to review every child who is looked after. Similarly, children who are accommodated under

s. 20 CA89 with parental agreement are required to have regular reviews whilst they remain looked after by the local authority.

Supervision order
The criteria for a supervision order are exactly the same as with an application for a care order. The question for the local authority is, if the threshold criteria is met, how will the making of a supervision order be better for the child than the making of no order? The making of a supervision order does not confer parental responsibility on the local authority so the parents retain full parental responsibility. The making of a supervision order does allow the local authority to retain a statutory role in terms of visiting the child and being informed of any changes in respect of the child. The role is to advise, assist and befriend the child (s. 35 (1)(a) CA89). Once made, the supervision order lasts for 12 months. The order may be extended for up to a maximum of three years, but this must be done by an application to extend.

Threshold criteria
This is the test which must be satisfied before the court can make either a care or supervision order in favour of the local authority.

UN Convention on the Rights of the Child
This treaty provides a guarantee of rights to children and young people in the UK, including the right, depending on the age and level of understanding of the child or young person, to express their views and to be listened to.

Welfare principle
'*When a court determines any question with respect to—(a) the upbringing of a child; or (b) the administration of a child's property or the application of any income arising from it, the child's welfare shall be the court's paramount consideration.*' (s. 1(1) CA89)

BIBLIOGRAPHY

Aldgate, J (1989) *Using Written Agreements with Children and Families* (London: FRG)

Aldgate J and J Simmonds (eds) (1988) *Direct Work with Children: A Guide for Social Work Practitioners* (London: Batsford)

Arnold, E (1987) *Whose Child? The Report of the Panel Appointed to Inquire into the Death of Tyra Henry* (London: London Borough of Lambeth)

Ashley, C (2008) Social Care Experts Blog, 29 October 2008 www.communitycare.co.uk/blogs/social-care-experts-blog/2008/10/lost-in-the-short-cuts/

Barker, J (1998) 'Extending the scope of child protection training' 7(4) *Child Abuse Review* 287–93

Barlow J and J Scott (2010) *Safeguarding in the 21st Century: Where to Now?* (Tomes: Research in Practice)

Beckett, C, J Dickens and S Bailey (2013) *Concluding Care Proceedings in 26 Weeks: Report of the Evaluation of the Tri-borough Pilot Project* (Norwich: Centre for Research on Children and Families/University of East Anglia)

Blacklaws, C (2009) 'Cafcass and the family justice system are failing vulnerable children' www.lawgazette.co.uk/opinion/comment/CAFCASS-and-the-family-justice-system-are-failing-vulnerable-children

Blacklaws, C and K Lickorish Quinn (2010) 'The revised PLO: a long road ahead' *Family Law Week* 5 September 2010 www.familylawweek.co.uk/site.aspx?i=ed65153

Blom-Cooper, J, L Brown, B Marshall, P Mason and M Beal (1985) *A Child in Trust: The Report of the Panel of Enquiry into the Circumstances Surrounding the Death of Jasmine Beckford* (London: London Borough of Brent)

Bostock, L, S Bairstow, S Fish and F MacLeod (2005) *Managing Risk and Minimising Mistakes in Services to Children and Families* (London: Social Care Institute for Excellence)

Brandon, M, S Bailey, P Belderson, R Gardner, P Sidebottom, J Dodsworth, C Warren and J Black (2009) *Understanding Serious Case Reviews and their Impact: A Biennial Analysis of Serious Case Reviews 2005–2007* (London: DCSF/TSO)

Brandon, M and J Thoburn (2008) 'Safeguarding children in the UK: a longitudinal study of services to children suffering or likely to suffer significant harm' 13(4) *Child and Family Social Work* 365–77

Broadhurst, K (2007) 'Parental help-seeking and the moral order. notes for policy makers and parenting practitioners on "the first port of call" and "no one to turn to"' 12(6) *Sociological Research Online,* paper listed in the *International Bibliography on Membership Categorisation Analysis* www.socresonline.org.uk/12/6/4.html

Broadhurst, K (2009) 'Safeguarding children through parenting support: how does every parent matter?' in K Broadhurst, C Grover and J Jamieson (eds) *Critical Perspectives on Safeguarding Children* (Oxford: Wiley-Blackwell)

Broadhurst, K, G Grover and J Jamieson (2009) 'Introduction' in K Broadhurst, G Grover and J Jamieson (eds) *Critical Perspectives on Safeguarding Children* (Oxford: Wiley-Blackwell)

Broadhurst, K, G Grover and J Jamieson (2009) 'Conclusion' in K Broadhurst, G Grover and J Jamieson (eds) *Critical Perspectives on Safeguarding Children* (Oxford: Wiley-Blackwell)

Broadhurst, K and K E Holt (2010) 'Partnership and the limits of procedure: prospects for relationships between parents and professionals under the new Public Law Outline' 15 *Child and Family Social Work* 97–106

Broadhurst, K and K E Holt (2012) 'Involving the Family Court Advisor in pre-proceedings practice – initial lessons from the Coventry and Warwickshire pilot' *Family Law Week* www.familylawweek.co.uk/site.aspx?i=ed97110

Broadhurst, K, K E Holt and P Doherty (2011) 'Accomplishing parental engagement in child protection practice? A qualitative analysis of parent–professional work under the Public Law Outline' 12(2) *Qualitative Social Work: Research and Practice* 158–78

Broadhurst, K, K E Holt, N Kelly and P Doherty (2013) *Coventry and Warwickshire Pre-proceedings Pilot: Final Report* (London: Cafcass)

Broadhurst, K, D Wastell, S White, C Hall, S Peckover, K Thompson, A Pithouse and D Davey (2010) 'Performing initial assessment: identifying the latent conditions for error in local authority children's services' 40(2) *British Journal of Social Work* 352–70 doi:10.1093/bjsw/bcn162

Broadhurst, K, S White, S Fish, E Munro, K Fletcher and H Lincoln (2010) *Ten Pitfalls and How To Avoid Them: What Research Tells Us* (London: NSPCC)

Brophy, J (2006) *Care Proceedings under the Children Act 1989: A Research Review* Research Series 06 (London: DCA/TSO)

Brown, H (2003) *Safeguarding Adults and Children with Disabilities against Abuse* (Strasbourg: Council of Europe Publishing)

Buchanan, A (1994) *Partnership in Practice: The Children Act 1989* (Avebury: Ashgate)

Bunting, L and C Reid (2005) 'Reviewing child deaths – learning from the American experience' XIV *Child Abuse Review* 82–96

Butler-Sloss, E J (1988) *Report of the Inquiry into Child Abuse in Cleveland 1987* Cmnd 412 (London: HMSO)

Calder, M C and M Barratt (1997) 'Inter-agency perspectives on core group practice' 11(4) *Children and Society* 209–21

Children and Family Court Advisory and Support Service (2006*) The Work of the Independent Reviewing Officer: A Report of a Survey of Local Authorities about the Application of Section 118 of the Adoption and Children Act 2002* (London: Cafcass)

Children and Family Court Advisory and Support Service (2012) 'Care demand: latest figures for June 2012' www.cafcass.gov.uk/pdf/June% 202012%20care%20demand%20update%20Final.pdf

Cicchetti, D and K Valentino (2006) 'An ecological transactional perspective on child maltreatment: failure of the average expectable environment and its influence upon child development' in D Cicchetti and D J Cohen (eds), *Developmental Psychopathology: Volume 3 Risk, Disorder, and Adaptation* 2nd edn (New York: Wiley)

Committee of Inquiry into the Care and Supervision Provided in Relation to Maria Colwell (1974) *Report of the Committee of Inquiry into the Care and Supervision Provided by Local Authorities and Other Agencies in Relation to Maria Colwell and the Co-ordination Between Them* (chair T G Field-Fisher) (London: HMSO)

Cooper, A (2005) 'Surface and depth in the Victoria Climbié Inquiry Report' 10(1) *Child and Family Social Work* 1–9

Corby, B, M Miller and L Young (1996) 'Parental participation in child protection work: rethinking the rhetoric' 25 *British Journal of Social Work* 475–92

Curtis, M (1946) *Report of the Care of Children Committee* (chair Myra Curtis) Cmd 6922 (London: HMSO)

Davis, G (1998) *Partisans and Mediators* (Oxford: Clarendon Press)

Davis, G, S Cretney and J Collins (1994) *Simple Quarrels: Negotiations and Adjudication in Divorce* (Oxford: Clarendon Press)

Davis, L (2007) *See You in Court: A Social Worker's Guide to Presenting Evidence in Care Proceedings* (London: Jessica Kingsley)

Davis, L (2009) *The Social Worker's Guide to Children and Families Law* (London: Jessica Kingsley)

Davy, C (2010) *Children's Participation in Decision-making: A Summary Report on Progress Made up to 2010* (London: NCB Participation Works)

De'Ath, E and G Pugh (eds) (1985–1986) *Partnership Papers* (London: National Children's Bureau)

Department for Children, Schools and Families (2007) *Review of Section 58 of the Children Act 2004* (London: TSO)

Department for Children, Schools and Families (2008) *The Children Act 1989 Guidance and Regulations Volume 1: Court Orders* (London: TSO)

Department for Children, Schools and Families (2010) *Working Together to Safeguard Children: A Guide to Inter-agency Working to Safeguard and Promote the Welfare of Children* (London: TSO)

Department for Constitutional Affairs (2006a) *Review of Childcare Proceedings in England and Wales* (London: DCA)

Department for Education (2011) *A Child-Centred System: The Government Response to the Munro Review* (London: TSO)

Department for Education (2013) *Working Together to Safeguard Children* (London: HMSO)

Department for Education and Skills (2003a) *Every Child Matters* (London: DfES)

Department for Education and Skills (2003b) *Keeping Children Safe* (Norwich: HMSO)

Department for Education and Skills (2007) *Care Matters: Time for Change* (London: TSO)

Department of Health (1988) *Protecting Children: A Guide for Social Workers Undertaking a Comprehensive Assessment* (London: HMSO)

Department of Health (1989) *The Care of Children: Principles and Practice in Regulations and Guidance* (London: HMSO)

Department of Health (1990) *An Introduction to the Children Act 1989* (London: HMSO)

Department of Health (1995) *Child Protection: Messages from Research* (London: HMSO)

Department of Health (2000) *Framework for the Assessment of Children in Need and their Families* (London: HMSO)

Department of Health (2003) *The Victoria Climbié Inquiry: Report of an Inquiry by Lord Laming* (London: HMSO)

Department of Health (2006) *Working Together to Safeguard Children: A Guide to Interagency Working to Safeguard and Promote the Welfare of Children* (London: HMSO)

Department of Health and Social Security (1985a) *Review of Child Care Law: Report to Ministers of an Interdepartmental Working Party* (London: HMSO)

Department of Health and Social Security (1985b) *Place of Safety and Interim Care Orders: Review of Child Care Law* (London: HMSO)

Easen, P, M Atkins and A Dyson (2000) 'Inter-professional collaboration and conceptualisations of practice' 14 *Children and Society* 355–67

Edwards, S and A Halpern (1992) 'Parental responsibility: an instrument of social policy' 22 *Family Law* 113–18

Eekelaar, J (2011) '"Not of the highest importance": family justice under threat' 33(4) *Journal of Social Welfare and Family Law* 311–17

Fahlberg, V I (1981) *Attachment and Separation* (London: British Association for Adoption and Fostering)

Fahlberg, V I (1991) *A Child's Journey through Placement* (London: British Association for Adoption and Fostering)

Family Rights Group (2009) *Professional Advocacy Services, Principles and Standards* (London: FRG)

Farmer, E and M Owen (1995) *Decision-making, Intervention and Outcome in Child Protection Work* (London: HMSO)

Farrell, A (2001) 'Legislative responsibility for child protection and human rights in Queensland' 6(1) *Australia and New Zealand Journal of Law and Education* 15–24

Featherstone, B (2009) *Contemporary Fathering: Theory, Policy and Practice* (Bristol: Policy Press)

Featherstone, B, K Broadhurst and K E Holt (2011) 'Thinking systemically–thinking politically: building strong partnerships with children and families in the context of rising inequality' *British Journal of Social Work* doi:10.1093/bjsw/bcr080

Featherstone, B and C Fraser (2012) '"I'm just a mother, I'm nothing special, they're all professionals": parental advocacy as an aid to parental engagement' 17(2) *Child and Family Social Work* 244–53

Featherstone, B, C Fraser, C Ashley and P Ledward (2011) 'Advocacy for parents and carers involved with children's services: making a difference to working in partnership?' 16(3) *Child and Family Social Work* 266–75

Featherstone, B, C A Hooper, J Scourfield and J Taylor (eds) (2010) *Gender and Child Welfare in Society* (Chichester: Wiley)

Featherstone, B, K Morris and S White (2013) 'A marriage made in hell: early intervention meets child protection' *British Journal of Social Work* doi:10.1093/bjsw/bct052

Ferguson, H (2010) 'Walks, home visits and atmospheres: risk and the everyday practices and mobilities of social work and child protection' 40 *British Journal of Social Work* 1100–17

Ferguson, H (2011) *Child Protection Practice* (Basingstoke: Palgrave Macmillan)

Fish, S, E Munro and S Bairstow (2008) *Learning Together to Safeguard Children: Developing a Multi-agency Systems Approach for Case Reviews* (London: Social Care Institute for Excellence)

France, A, E Munro and A Waring (2010) *The Evaluation of Arrangements for Effective Operation of the New Local Safeguarding Children Boards in England* (Loughborough: Centre for Research in Social Policy and Centre for Child and Family Research Loughborough University)

Freeman, D A (1992) *Children, their Families and the Law: Working with the Children Act* (London: Macmillan)

Freeman, P and J Hunt (1998) *Parental Perspectives on Care Proceedings* (London: TSO)

Galligan, D J (1986) *Discretionary Powers* (Oxford: Oxford University Press)

Gibbons, J, B Gallagher, C Bell and D Gordon (1995) *Development after Physical Abuse in Early Childhood* (London: HMSO)

Gillen, S (2009) 'Care proceedings and applications post-Baby P' *Community Care Online* www.communitycare.co.uk/Articles/2009/01/14/110406/how-the-public-law-outline-is-affecting-care-cases-in-the-wake-of-baby.html

Gilligan, P, M Manby and C Pickburn (2011) 'Fathers' involvement in children's services: exploring local and national issues in "Moorlandstown"' 42(3) *British Journal of Social Work* 500–18

Gore, S (2012) 'Norgrove: the response considered' *Family Law Week* 12 December 2012 www.familylawweek.co.uk/site.aspx?i=ed95674

Gray, B (2009) 'Befriending excluded families in Tower Hamlets: the emotional labour of family support workers in cases of child protection and family support' 39(6) *British Journal of Social Work* 990–1007

Grover, C (2008) *Crime and Inequality* (Cullompton: Willan)

Hall, C, N Parton, S Peckover and S White (2010) 'Child-centric ICTs and the fragmentation of child welfare practice in England' 39(3) *Journal of Social Policy* 393–413

Harding, J, E Mc C Milton and L Blom-Cooper (1987) *A Child in Mind: Protection of Children in a Responsible Society – The Report of the Commission of Inquiry into the Circumstances Surrounding the Death of Kimberley Carlile: Presented to the London Borough of Greenwich and the Greenwich Health Authority by Members of the Commission of Inquiry* (Greenwich: London Borough of Greenwich)

Hardy, B, A Turrell and G Winstow (1992) *Innovations in Community Care Management* (Aldershot: Avebury)

Harlow, E and S Shardlow (2006) 'Safeguarding children: challenges to the effective operation of core groups' 11 *Child and Family Social Work* 65–72

Harwin, J (1992) 'Child protection and the role of the social worker under the Children Act 1989' in M Parry (ed.) *The Children Act 1989: Conflict and Compromise* (Hull: Hull University Law School)

Hester, M, C Pearson, N Harwin and H Abrahams (2006) *Making an Impact: Children and Domestic Violence: A Reader* (London: Jessica Kingsley)

Hindley, N, P G Ramchandani and D P H Jones (2006) 'Risk factors for recurrence of maltreatment: a systematic review' *Archive of Diseases in Childhood* doi:10.1136/adc.2005.085639

Holland, S and J Scourfield (2004) 'Liberty and respect in child protection' 24(1) *British Journal of Social Work* 17–32

Holt, K E and N Kelly (2012a) 'Administrative decision making in child-care work: exploring issues of judgement and decision making in the context of human rights and its relevance for social workers and managers' *British Journal of Social Work* doi:10.1093/bjsw/bcs168

Holt, K E and N Kelly (2012b) 'Rhetoric and reality surrounding care proceedings: family justice under strain' *Journal of Social Welfare and Family Law.* http://dx.doi.org/10.1080/09649069.2012.718531

Holt, K E, N Kelly, K Broadhurst and P Doherty (2013) *Liverpool Pre-proceedings Pilot: Interim Report* (London: Cafcass)

Holt, K E, N Kelly, P Doherty and K Broadhurst (2013) 'Access to justice for families? Legal advocacy for parents where children are on the "edge of care": an English case study' *Journal of Social Welfare and Family Law* doi:10.1093/bjsw/bcs168

Home Office (1989) 'The duties and powers of police under the Children Act 1989' Home Office Circular 44/2003

Home Office (1991) *Working Together: A Guide to Arrangements for Interagency Cooperation for the Protection of Children from Abuse* (London: Home Office)

Home Office (2006) *Achieving Best Evidence in Criminal Proceedings: Guidance for Vulnerable or Intimidated Witnesses, Including Children* (London: Home Office)

Hopkins, G (1998) *Plain English for Social Services: A Guide to Better Communication* (Lyme Regis: Russell House)

House of Commons Justice Committee (2012) *Pre-legislative Scrutiny of the Children and Families Bill: Fourth Report of Session 2012–2013: Volume I: Report together with Formal Minutes, Oral and Written Evidence* (London: TSO)

Horwath, J and T Morrison (2007) 'Developing multi-agency partnerships to serve vulnerable children and their families' 31(1) *Child Abuse and Neglect* 55–69

Hudson, B (2000) 'Interagency collaboration: a sceptical view' in A Brechin, H Brown and M A Eby (eds) *Critical Practice in Health and Social Care* (London: Sage and Open University) 255–74

Hudson, B, B Hardy, M Henwood and G Wistow (2003) 'In pursuit of interagency collaboration in the public sector: what is the contribution of theory and research?' in J Reynolds, J Henderson, J Seden, J C Worth and A Bullman (eds) *The Managing Care Reader* (London: Routledge) 232–41

Hunt, J, A Macleod and C Thomas (1999) *The Last Resort: Child Protection, the Courts and the 1989 Children Act* (London: TSO)

Iwaniec, D, T Donaldson and M Allweiss (2004) 'The plight of neglected children: social work and judicial decision-making and management of neglected cases' 16(4) *Child and Family Law Quarterly* 423–36

Jessiman, P, P Keogh and J Brophy (2009) *An Early Process Evaluation of the Public Law Outline in Family Courts* MoJ Research Series 10/09 (London: MoJ)

Judicial Review Team (2005) *Thematic Review of the Protocol for Judicial Case Management in Public Law Children Act Cases* (London: TSO)

Judiciary of England and Wales (2012) *The Family Justice Modernisation Programme: The Third Update from Mr Justice Ryder*, March 2012 www.judiciary.gov.uk/Resources/JCO/Documents/Reports/family_newsletter3.pdf

Kaganas, F (1995) 'Partnership under the Children Act 1989: an overview' in F Kaganas, M King and C Piper (eds) *Legislating for Harmony* (London: Jessica Kingsley)

Kaganas, F, M King and C Piper (eds) (1995) *Legislating for Harmony* (London: Jessica Kingsley)

Kelly, N (2002) *Decision-making in Child Protection Practice*, PhD thesis, Huddersfield University

Khan, A (2006) 'Child care protocol: how is it working in practice?' *Family Law Week* www.familylawweek.co.uk/site.aspx?i=ed1591

Klug, F (2007) 'A bill of rights: what for?' in C Bryant (ed.) *Towards a New Constitutional Settlement* (London: The Smith Institute)

Lefevre, M (2010) *Communicating with Children and Young People: Making a Difference* (Bristol: Policy Press)

Lindley, B (1994a) *Families in Court: Final Report – A Qualitative Study of the Experiences of the Court Process in Care and Supervision Proceedings under the Children Act* (London: FRG)

Lindley, B (1994b) *On the Receiving End: Families' Experience of the Court Process in Care and Supervision Proceedings under the Children Act 1989* (London: FRG)

Lutman, E and E Farmer (2013) 'What contributes to outcomes for neglected children who are reunified with their parents? Findings from a five-year follow-up study' 43(3) *British Journal of Social Work* 559–78

Lyon, C (2003) *Child Abuse* 3rd edn (London: Jordan)

Maclean, M and J Eekelaar (2010) *Family Law Advocacy: How Barristers Help the Victims of Family Failure* (Oxford: Hart)

Maclean, M and J Kurczewski (2011) *Making Family Law: A Socio-Legal Account of Legislative Process in England and Wales, 1985 to 2010* (Oxford: Hart)

Masson, J M (2008) 'Controlling costs and maintaining services: the reform of legal aid fees for care proceedings' 20(4) *Child and Family Law Quarterly* 425–48

Masson, J M (2010) 'A new approach to care proceedings' 15 *Child and Family Social Work* 369–79

Masson, J M (2011a) 'Public child law: a service priority?' 33 *Journal of Social Welfare and Family Law* 361–77

Masson, J M (2011b) 'Reforming care proceedings: a socio-legal perspective' in M Thorpe and W Tyzack (eds) *Dear David: A Memo to the Norgrove Committee from the Dartington Conference 2011* (London: Jordan) 79–87

Masson, J M, J Dickens, K F Bader and J Young (2013) *Partnership by Law? The Pre-proceedings Process for Families on the Edge of Care Proceedings* (Bristol: School of Law, University of Bristol)

Masson, J M, J Pearce and K F Bader (2011) 'Just following instructions? The representation of parents in care proceedings' http://ssrn.com/abstract= 1844663 or http://dx.doi.org/10.2139/ssrn.1844663

Masson, J M, J Pearce and K F Bader (with O Joyner, J Marsden and D Westlake) (2008) *Care Profiling Study* (London: Ministry of Justice)

McKeigue, B and C Beckett (2008) 'Squeezing the toothpaste tube: will tackling court delay result in pre-court delay in its place?' *British Journal of Social Work* doi:10.1093/bjsw/bcn119

Melucci, A (1996) *The Playing Self: Person and Meaning in the Planetary Society* (Cambridge: Cambridge University Press)

Milham, S, R Bullock, K Hosie and M Little (1986) *Lost in Care: The Problems of Maintaining Links between Children in Care and their Families* (Aldershot: Gower)

Ministry of Justice (2003) *Protocol for the Judicial Management of Public Law Child Care Cases* (London: MoJ)

Ministry of Justice (2008) *Public Law Outline* (London: MoJ)

Ministry of Justice (2011a) *Family Justice Review: Final Report* (London: MoJ)

Ministry of Justice (2011b) *Family Justice Review: Interim Report* (London: MoJ)

Ministry of Justice and Department for Education (2012) *The Government Response to the Family Justice Review: A System with Children and Families at its Heart* (London: TSO)

Morris, K (2012) 'Thinking family? The complexities for family engagement in care and protection' 42(5) *British Journal of Social Work* 906–20

Munby, Justice (2009) 'Family advocacy within local authority decision making processes' address by Mr Justice Munby to the FRG Conference: Professional Family Advocacy and Safeguarding Children, London, June 2009

Munby, Justice (President of the Family Division) (2013) 'View from the President's chambers (6): the process of reform – latest developments' (MOJ: London)

Munro, E (2010) *Munro Review of Child Protection: Part One – A Systems Analysis* (London: DfE)

Munro, E (2011) *The Munro Report of Child Protection: Final Report – A Child-Centred System* (London: DfE)

Murphy, M (2004) *Developing Collaborative Relationships in Interagency Child Protection Work* (Lyme Regis: Russell House)

Nagalro (February 2012) *Government Response to the Family Justice Review Weakens Safeguards for Children* www.nagalro.com/feeds/news/government-response-weakens-court-safeguards-for-children.aspx

Nelken, D (1987) 'The use of "contracts" as a social work technique' 40 *Current Legal Problems* 207–32

Office of the Children's Commissioner (2013) *A Child Rights Impact Assessment of Budget Decisions: Including the 2013 Budget, and the Cumulative Impact of Tax-benefit Reforms and Reductions in Spending on Public Services 2010–2015* (London: Children's Commissioner)

Ofsted (2011) *Ages of Concern: Learning Lessons from Serious Case Reviews –A Thematic Report of Ofsted's Evaluation of Serious Case Reviews from 1 April 2007 to 31 March 2011* (London: Ofsted)

Ofsted (2012) *Protecting Disabled Children: Thematic Inspection* (London: Ofsted)

Packman, J, J Randall and N Jacques (1986) *Who Needs Care? Social-Work Decisions about Children* (Oxford: Basil Blackwell)

Parton, N (2004) 'From Maria Caldwell to Victoria Climbié: reflections on public inquiries into child abuse a generation apart' 13 *Child Abuse Review* 80–94

Pugh, G, G Aplin, E De'Ath and M Moxon (1987) *Partnership in Action: Working with Parents in a Pre-school Centre* (London: National Children's Bureau)

Pugh, G and E De'Ath (1985) *The Needs of Parents* (London: Macmillan)

Reder, P and S Duncan (1999) *Lost Innocents: A Follow-up Study of Fatal Child Abuse* (London: Routledge)

Reder, P, S Duncan and M Gray (1993) *Beyond Blame: Child Abuse Tragedies Revisited* (London: Routledge.)

Reissman, C and L Quinney (2005) 'Narrative in social work: a critical review' 4(4) *Qualitative Social Work* 391–412

Seebohm Report (1969) *Social Services: The Seebohm Report*, HL Deb 29 January 1969, vol. 298, cols 1168–93

Sidebotham, P (2012) 'What do serious case reviews achieve?' 97(3) *Archives of Disease in Childhood* 189–92

Sinclair, R and R Bullock (2002) *Learning from Past Experience: A Review of Serious Case Reviews* (London: DoH)

Swain, P A (2009) *In the Shadow of the Law* (Sydney NSW: Federation Press)

Thoburn, J (2012) 'Achieving successful returns from care: what makes reunification work?' 42(5) *British Journal of Social Work* 995–97

Thoburn, J, A Chand and J Procter (2005) *Child Welfare Services for Minority Ethnic Families: The Research Reviewed* (London: Jessica Kingsley)

Thoburn, J, A Lewis and D Shemmings (1995) *Paternalism or Partnership? The Involvement of Family Members in Child Protection* (London: HMSO)

Thompson, N (2009) *Understanding Social Work: Preparing for Practice* (Basingstoke: Palgrave Macmillan)

Wallace, I and L Bunting (2007) *An Examination of Local, National and International Arrangements for the Mandatory Reporting of Child Abuse: The Implications for Northern Ireland* (Belfast: NSPCC Northern Ireland Policy and Research Unit)

Wastell, D, S White, K Broadhurst, C Hall, S Peckover and A Pithouse (2010) 'Children's services in the iron cage of performance management: street level bureaucracy and the spectre of Švejkism' 19 *International Journal of Social Welfare* 310–20

Welbourne, P (2008) 'Safeguarding children on the edge of care: policy for keeping children safe after the review of the child care proceedings system, Care Matters and the Carter Review of Legal Aid' (20(3) *Child and Family Law Quarterly* 335–58

White, S and K Broadhurst (2009) 'Raging against the machine' (January) *Professional Social Work* 8–10

White, S, K Broadhurst and D Wastell (2008) 'Shortfalls of IT in children's services' *Community Care Magazine* 11 December 2008 www.community-care.co.uk/Articles/2008/12/11/110219/the-shortfalls-of-it-in-childrens-services.html

White, S, D Wastell, K Broadhurst and C Hall (2010) 'When policy o'erleaps itself: the tragic tale of the Integrated Children's System' 30 *Critical Social Policy* 405–29

Woodhouse, S (1995) 'Child protection and working in partnership with parents' in F Kaganas, M King and C Piper (eds) *Legislating for Harmony* (London: Jessica Kingsley)

INDEX